Internet Explorer on the Intern

A practical step-by-step guide to using your browser

HOW TO COPY PICTURES (MULTIPLES)

GO INTO WORD PAD

CLICK PICTURE SYMBLE

GO INTO PICTURE LIBRARY

SELECT PICTURE

CLICK ON CORNER OF PICTURE TO

MINIMISE.

PRINT

Internet Handbooks

Other titles in preparation

Internet
Explorer
on the internet

A practical step-by-step guide to using your browser

Kye Valongo

www.internet-handbooks.co.uk

Other Internet Handbooks by the same author

Free Stuff on the Internet
Discussion Forums on the Internet
Getting Started on the Internet
Using Email on the Internet
Using Netscape on the Internet
Where to Find It on the Internet
Your Privacy on the Internet

First published in 2001 by Internet Handbooks Ltd, Plymbridge House, Estover Road, Plymouth PL6 7PY, United Kingdom.

Customer services tel:	(01752) 202301
Orders fax:	(01752) 202333
Customer services email:	cservs@plymbridge.com
Distributors web site:	www.plymbridge.com
Internet Handbooks web site:	www.internet-handbooks.co.uk

Note: The contents of this book are offered for the purposes of general guidance only and no liability can be accepted for any loss or expense incurred as a result of relying in particular circumstances on statements made in this book. Readers are advised to check the current position with the appropriate authorities before entering into personal arrangements.

Case studies in this book are entirely fictional and any resemblance to real persons or organisations is entirely coincidental.

Typeset by PDQ Typesetting, Newcastle-under-Lyme.
Printed and bound by The Cromwell Press Ltd, Trowbridge, Wiltshire.

Contents

. . . .

List of illustrations

Preface

. . . .

The world wide web is all about information. At the same time, it is about more than just information − it is a place where we can each communicate and potentially share information with anyone on earth. It can help people of all different kinds to communicate with one another and work together by removing misunderstandings. It even has the potential, if governments allow it, to encourage world peace.

Internet Explorer probably needs little introduction. Essentially, it is a tool that allows you easily to access this world wide web on your computer − in short, it is a web browser. A browser acts as a window to the web and lets you take part in the many activities that are available, such as viewing web sites or chatting to people in discussion groups. Special components in the Internet Explorer package allow you to use email and newsgroups; others even enable you design and publish your own web site − all for free. Internet Explorer is at present the most widely used browser, a product of Microsoft.

This guide concentrates on Internet Explorer version 5, which is at present the latest available, and is best used alongside your computer. The information in these pages is presented in a condensed form to help you master the fundamentals of Internet Explorer without having to wade through pages and pages of irrelevant explanation. You can work through from start to finish using the step-by-step approach, or you can just dip into it with the aid of the contents list, index and glossary.

It is assumed that if you know what Internet Explorer, and the internet are, then you do not need help in how to use the mouse, how to open menus, and so on. At the same time, an attempt has been made to cut out the unnecessary jargon, on a strictly 'need to know' basis. If you don't need to know the long words, why use them!

Apologies to left-handed readers − or those who have set their mouse to be left-handed − for use of the expression 'right-click the mouse' when the opposite may be the case for them.

Happy browsing!

Kye Valongo

kyevalongo@internet-handbooks.co.uk

1 Internet Explorer basics

In this chapter we will explore:

▶ *installing Internet Explorer*
▶ *uninstalling Internet Explorer*
▶ *connecting and disconnecting*
▶ *the Internet Explorer toolbar*
▶ *key shortcuts*
▶ *getting help*

. . . .

An Internet Explorer installation normally requires a computer with the following specifications:

1. At least 16 megabytes of RAM (random access memory).

2. Between 7 and 30 megabytes of hard disk space.

3. A Microsoft Windows operating system – 3.x, 95, 98, NT 4.0 or better.

Most computers will already have a browser installed – most likely Internet Explorer. If you have no browser, or if you have a different one and you

Fig. 1. Internet Explorer download page. The Microsoft download site has lots of software that you can download, not just Internet Explorer 5. It is well worth looking around for other interesting programs, including games for example.

would like to change to Internet Explorer, there are a couple of ways you can obtain it.

Microsoft Internet Explorer 5 is free to download from Microsoft's own web site (figure 1). The address is:

http://www.microsoft.com/windows/ie

However, you will find it far easier, and very much quicker, to visit your newsagent and buy one of the many internet magazines that supply Internet Explorer on a cover CD.

Alternatively, you can obtain one of the many free CDs that ISPs such as Freeserve, Virgin Net and many others supply either to the larger stores, or direct. That way, you will not need to spend an hour or more downloading the huge files that comprise Internet Explorer 5.

▶ *ISP (internet service provider)* – The company that provides you with access to the internet, usually via your telephone line. Your ISP will usually also provide your internet software, and make other services available to you online (news, chat etc).

You may want to install IE 5 over a previous version of Internet Explorer, such as version 3 or 4. If you do, the process is simple. Internet Explorer 5 even saves your existing browser settings and list of Favorites.

If you are installing from a CD given to you by an ISP, the particular details of the installation may differ from what is explained below. This is because ISPs often customise the way Internet Explorer installs itself. However, the following steps should be correct for most variations.

How to download and install Internet Explorer 5

1. Visit the following web page and Click Download Now at the top of the page:

   http://www.microsoft.com/windows/ie/download/ie55.htm

2. Choose 'Run this program from its current location' and click OK.

3. Click Yes if asked whether you would like to install and run Microsoft Internet Explorer 5.5 and Tools.

4. Accept the License Agreement. Then click Next to begin the installation process.

Installation is more or less the same as for a CD installation from this point on, but it can take an hour or more if done online. If for any reason your internet connection is interrupted, you will have to start this time-consuming process all over again. A window will show the progress of the download (figure 2).

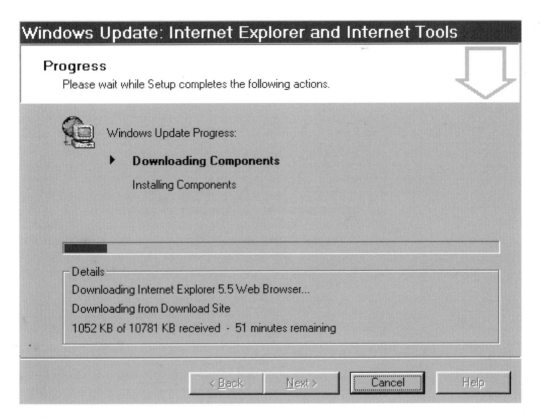

Windows Update: Internet Explorer and Internet Tools

Progress
Please wait while Setup completes the following actions.

Windows Update Progress:

▶ **Downloading Components**

Installing Components

─Details─
Downloading Internet Explorer 5.5 Web Browser...
Downloading from Download Site
1052 KB of 10781 KB received - 51 minutes remaining

< Back   Next >   Cancel   Help

The license agreement
You will first be asked to read and accept a license agreement. If you do not accept this, the installation cannot continue.

Installing components
Then a dialog box will ask you which components you want to install. Choosing Minimal Installation lets you exclude components you don't want to install. For example, you can choose to install the browser only. If you choose Typical Installation, the most commonly used components will be put on your computer.

Restarting your computer
When the main installation has finished, you will be prompted to restart your computer. Internet Explorer 5 will finish installing after your computer has restarted.

The Internet Connection Wizard
Once the installation has finished, start the Internet Connection Wizard (figure 3). To do this, double-click the Internet Explorer icon on your desktop. The Internet Explorer is one of the standard icons on your desktop (figure 4). Alternatively, open Start, Programs, then Internet Explorer. A series of dialog boxes will prompt you for information about your internet settings. Choose the options that apply to you.

Fig. 2. An Internet Explorer download in progress. This can easily take over an hour so the best time to do it is at the weekend. Even better, though, is to install if from a CD. Many ISPs offer free CDs that contain Internet Explorer – you don't have to sign up with the ISP to install Internet Explorer.

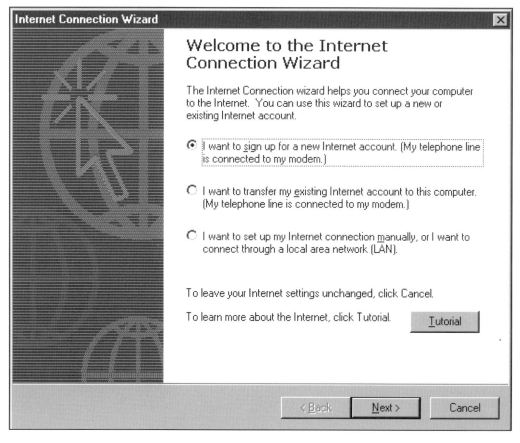

Fig. 3. The Internet Connection Wizard.

You will then see a screen called Set Up Your Internet Mail Account. This gives you the option of letting Internet Explorer set up your new Outlook Express mail client with your email information and preferences.

If you are setting up your email for the first time, you need to obtain information from your ISP before you set up the account. You will normally need to know:

1. your user name (email name), e.g. 'james.mcsmythe'

2. the name of your mailserver, e.g. mail.virgin.net

3. password

If you have one or more existing email accounts, your existing settings will be imported during the installation.

Fig. 4. The Internet Explorer is one of the standard icons on your desktop.

Network Neighborhood   My Computer   Internet Explorer   Recycle Bin

Uninstalling Internet Explorer 5

Although Internet Explorer is a great browser, you may later want to replace it with one of the others such as Opera, or Netscape Navigator. Uninstalling it will save valuable space on our hard drive. It may also prevent possible software conflicts with other browsers.

Add/Remove Programs
You can uninstall Internet Explorer using the Windows Control Panel's Add/Remove Programs tool (figure 5). Before you start doing so, close all other Windows programs. Then:

1. Select Start, Settings, Control Panel. Then double-click the Add/Remove Programs icon.

2. In the Add/Remove Programs Properties dialog box, select Microsoft Internet Explorer 5 and Internet Tools. Then click Add/Remove.

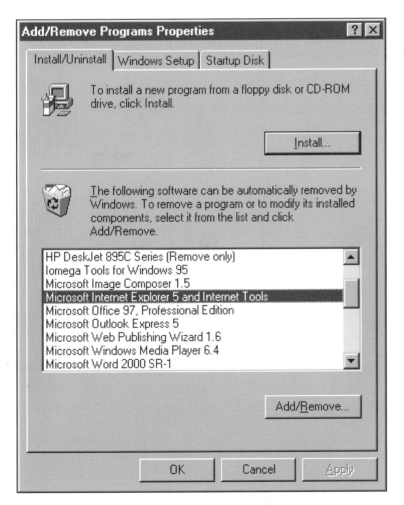

Fig. 5. Removing the Internet Explorer software from a computer.

Internet Explorer basics ....

Fig. 6. Uninstalling Internet Explorer 5 may not remove an earlier version of Internet Explorer so you may just want to keep it. When you install a new browser, it should change the file associations so that whenever you click on an HTML file, the new browser will open.

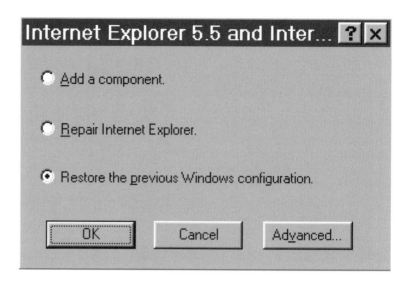

Fig. 7. Dial-up connection (FreeUK). When you start Internet Explorer, the Windows DUN window opens and asks you for your user name and password. You also have the option of saving your password. Don't use this facility if there is the slightest possibility that your computer could be used by someone other than you.

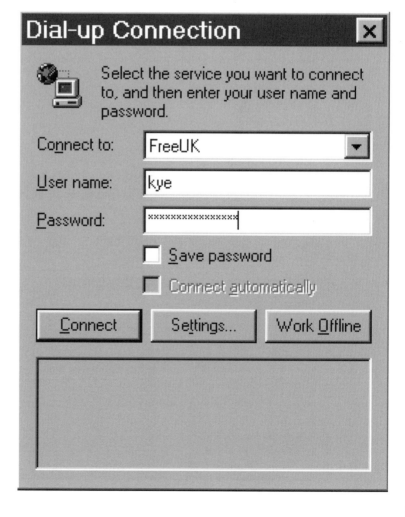

You will then be given several options (figure 6): Add a component, Repair Internet Explorer, or Restore the previous Windows configuration. Select the last option, then click OK. The uninstaller will remove the program in a few moments.

Reinstalling Windows 95 and 98
Knowing how to uninstall Internet Explorer 5 is essential should you ever want to reinstall Windows 95 on your computer. You must uninstall Internet Explorer 5 first. Otherwise, Windows may not start up after installation, or various Internet Explorer components may not work.

Windows 98 does not suffer from this problem. It can be reinstalled safely without having to uninstall Internet Explorer 5 first.

Connecting and disconnecting

Internet Explorer will be set up to connect to the internet for you whenever it starts. Click on the Internet Explorer icon on your desktop to start the browser and connect to the internet. When Internet Explorer tries to connect to the internet, it will start Windows Dial-Up Networking (Windows DUN, for short), and you will see a 'Connect to' window. Figures 7 and 8 show two examples: one where the ISP is FreeUK, the other where the ISP is Virgin Net.

If you have not yet signed up to an ISP, or if Internet Explorer is not configured to your ISP, the internet connection wizard will start to enable you to set up your existing ISP with Internet Explorer or open a new account.

Fig. 8. Dial-up connection (Virgin Net).

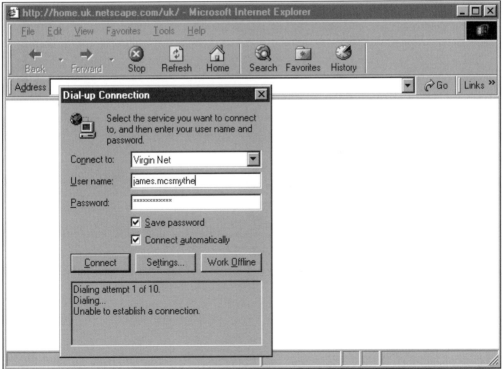

Internet Explorer basics ....

Once you are connected, the 'Connecting to' notice disappears and the Windows DUN window minimises to a small icon on your start menu (figure 9).

'Connected' icon

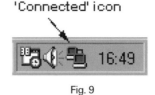

Fig. 9

If the connection fails

If for some reason, Internet Explorer does not connect to the internet, you will have to change the settings or connect manually. To configure (set up) Internet Explorer so it connects whenever you start it:

1. Open the Tools menu and select Internet Options.

2. Select the Connections tab.

3. Click on 'Always dial my default connection'.

To connect manually:

(a) Open My Computer and, in the Dial-Up Networking window.

(b) Click the connection for your ISP.

(c) Enter your name and password.

(d) Click Connect.

The 'Connecting to' window should now appear as your computer dials into the ISP's number.

Checking your Dial-Up Networking
If even this fails, you may not have Windows DUN installed or you may have to reinstall it. To make sure you have Dial-Up Networking installed:

1. Double-click My Computer on your desktop (figure 10). If you do not see an icon for Dial-Up Networking, then:

2. Open the Start menu, select Settings, then Add/Remove Programs.

3. Click Communications, and then Details.

4. Select the Dial-Up Networking check box, and click OK.

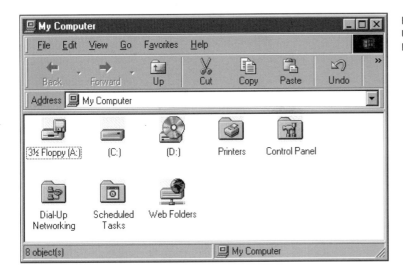

Fig. 10. Checking your Dial-Up Networking in Control Panel.

Disconnecting

To disconnect, simply right click on the icon on your Windows toolbar and select 'Disconnect' (figure 11).

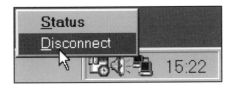

Fig. 11.

The Internet Explorer toolbar

Of all the ways of controlling Internet Explorer, the toolbar is probably the one you will want to use the most and it has all of the common commands on the one bar (figure 12). Later, you will learn how to customise the toolbar – and many other features of Internet Explorer. The main buttons are described below.

Fig. 12. Internet Explorer toolbars. The buttons on the toolbars will often be obscured for various reasons. Click the mouse cursor on the small black single and double arrows to view the hidden buttons.

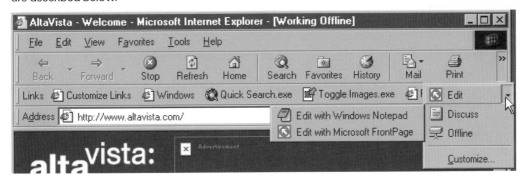

Internet Explorer basics ....

Forward and Back

When you have loaded one or more new pages, you can return to the earlier pages that you visited by clicking the Back button. When you want to return to the later pages, you can click the Forward button.

▶ *Tip* – Instead of clicking the Back button, you can press the BACK-SPACE key to move back a page.

Stop

Clicking on the Stop button stops the current page from loading. This is useful for slow loading pages, or if you suddenly find that you have entered the wrong URL (uniform resource locator, i.e. web site address).

Refresh

The Refresh button reloads the current page. Use this button if you want to check for fresh material added since the last time you visited, or if the page didn't load properly the first time.

Home

The Home button loads your home page. For an explanation of this term, see page 29.

Search

The Search button opens a search pane on the left side of your main window. For more about this see page 34.

Favorites

Clicking on the Favorites button opens your bookmarked web sites in a separate pane of your browser. For more about Favorites see page 29.

History

Clicking on the History button opens a pane listing the sites you've visited recently. You can revisit any of these sites just by clicking on them. For more about this see page 29.

Mail

Clicking on the Mail button opens your email program. For more about this see page 46.

Print

Clicking on the Print button prints out the current page (assuming you have a printer connected to your computer!).

Edit

If you have the web authoring software FrontPage Express installed, you will also have an Edit button (figure 13). This opens the current web page in FrontPage Express. For more about this see page 68.

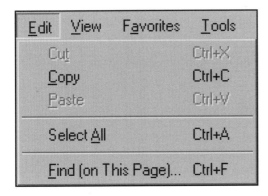

Fig. 13. You will see an Edit button if you also have
FrontPage installed for web page authoring.

Key shortcuts

The mouse is not the only way to control Internet Explorer. In fact it is often easier to use the keyboard for common actions.

▶ *Tip* – A key shortcut, such as Ctrl F, is often a combination of two keys. There is often confusion about how to press the two keys. It is simple: press the first key and keep it pressed while you tap the second key once. With Ctrl F (control F), for example, press the control key (usually the bottom left key with 'Ctrl' written on it), keep it pressed down and now tap the 'F' key once. Now let go of the control key. That should have opened the 'Find' dialog box in Internet Explorer.

Some of the more useful key shortcuts include:

Key	Command
F1	Use Internet Explorer help
F 5	Refresh the current web page
F 11	Use Internet Explorer in full screen mode
Ctrl O	Open a web page or a document on your computer
Ctrl F	Find some text on the current web page
Ctrl C	Copy the selected text or images from the current web page to the clipboard. (You can paste it into another program with Ctrl V)
Alt HOME	Go to your home page

For more on key shortcuts use Internet Explorer help.

19

Internet Explorer basics ....

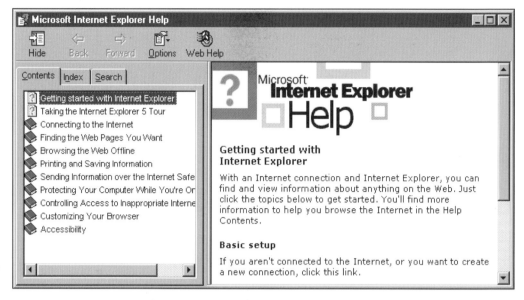

Fig. 14. Internet Explorer
help – contents and index.

Getting help

Once you have installed Internet Explorer, it offers many ways for you to
get help:

1. Press the F1 shortcut key while Internet Explorer is open.

2. Open the Help menu and select Contents and Index (figure 14).

3. Tip of the day, which displays helpful tips at the bottom of the brow-
    ser.

4. Open the Help menu and select Tour.

If you already have an internet connection, perhaps the most useful type
of help will be the online Tour. This takes you to the Microsoft web site and
gives you a guided tour of Internet Explorer from the basics to more
advanced features (figure 15).

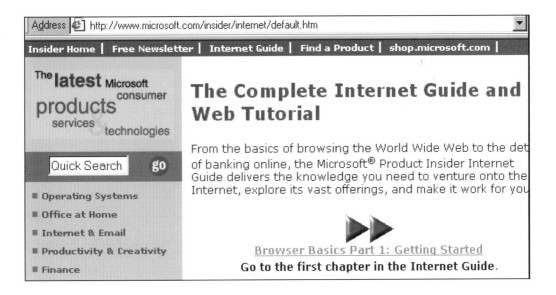

Fig. 15. Internet Explorer tour. The Microsoft tour is a good site to learn about Internet Explorer 5 while using it online, but there are plenty of options that will not use up your telephone bill.

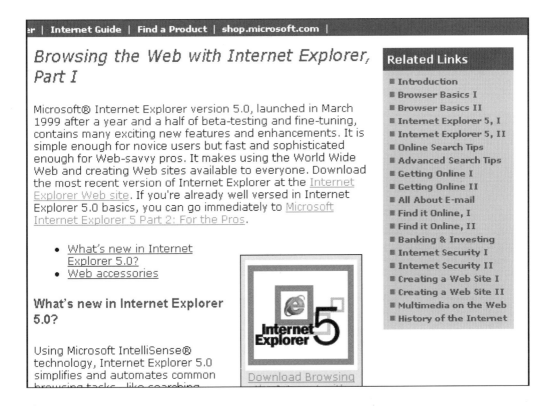

2 Using Internet Explorer online

In this chapter we will explore:

▶ *visiting your first site*

▶ *understanding links and addresses*

▶ *returning to sites that you have visited before*

▶ *the cache*

▶ *offline viewing*

▶ *searching for sites*

▶ *customising Internet Explorer*

▶ *the radio toolbar*

. . . .

Visiting your first site

Fig. 16. Clicking the Home icon on the Internet Explorer toolbar will load whichever 'home page' is specified in your browser. This will probably be the home page of your internet service provider (in this example, Virgin Net).

Viewing a web page is simplicity in itself. Most ISPs design their sites so that you can use them as a jump-off point to the internet each time you connect. They also customise your copy of Internet Explorer so that when you open it, it will generally load your ISP's home page.

Try it yourself: connect to the internet according to your ISP's instructions, then start your browser program. You should now be watching a web page appear as it is retrieved in stages. The text will become visible first followed, one by one, by the images. At the top of the browser window, you'll see a menu bar, a toolbar, and an address line that contains the address of the page you're presently viewing (figure 16).

▶ *Tip* – If the text on a site is all you are interested in, you can stop images and sounds from loading. Just click the Tools menu, Internet Options, select the Advanced tab, and turn off sounds and pictures. This will also make browsing much faster.

Every time a browser starts, it tries to find a page called the home page. Initially, the location of the home page is set by the browser manufacturer or your ISP and is usually one of the main pages of that company. Finding a different web site after the home page has loaded is also a simple matter.

All but the most basic web pages contain references or links (also referred to as hyperlinks) to pages on the same and on other web sites. These links contain information which tells your browser where the page referred to is located: its address. You click on a link with your mouse cursor, and the browser loads the page at that particular address.

Understanding links and addresses

Underlined text usually indicates that it is a link. Often these links are arranged in a menu system at one edge of a web page. A text link might look like this:

<u>Click Here for more info.</u>

Other links appear as buttons or images on the web page (figure 17).

Clicking on a link is easy – all you need to do is click and your browser will read the address contained in the link and load the page into your browser.

However, if you read about a site, for example on television or in a magazine, you will need to know its address yourself so that you can type it into the address box. The address of a web page is similar to that of someone's house. The address of a web page is called the URL (uniform resource locator) and is unique for each page, just as house

Fig. 17. Hyperlinks. It will be rare for you to have to type in the address of a web site. Mostly, you will be clicking on hyperlinks that are on an existing web page, as in this example Microsoft web page.

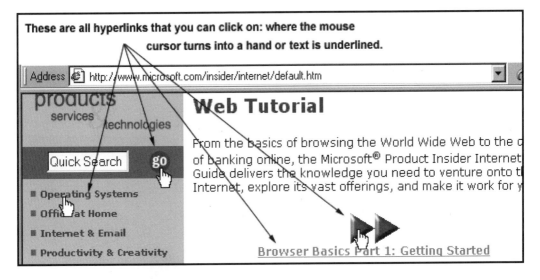

These are all hyperlinks that you can click on: where the mouse cursor turns into a hand or text is underlined.

Address 📧 http://www.microsoft.com/insider/internet/default.htm

products
services
technologies

Quick Search   go

■ Operating Systems
■ Office at Home
■ Internet & Email
■ Productivity & Creativity

Web Tutorial

From the basics of browsing the World Wide Web to the
of banking online, the Microsoft® Product Insider Internet
Guide delivers the knowledge you need to venture onto th
Internet, explore its vast offerings, and make it work for y

Browser Basics Part 1: Getting Started

Using Internet Explorer online...

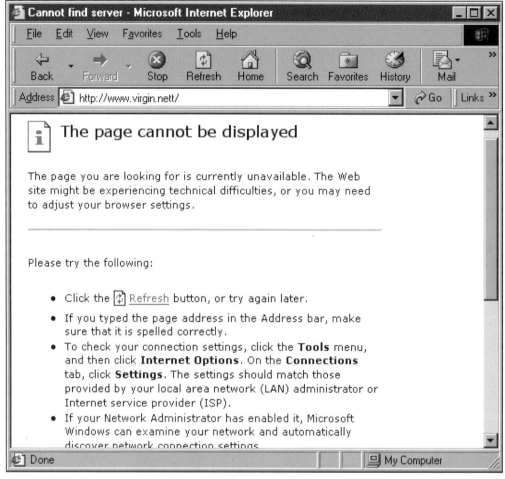

Fig. 18. An error message. In this case, the page could not be displayed correctly because there was a mistake in typing the URL – nett instead of net.

addresses are unique. If you type the address slightly wrongly, you will either find the wrong site or be shown an error message (figure 18).

▶ *URL* – uniform resource locator. This means the unique web address of a web page, image or other document on the internet.

An example of a simple URL is:

http://ukdirectory.com

It looks strange and makes little sense to the uninitiated. But if you study it, you will be able to make out the words 'directory' and 'UK' so you might guess that it is the URL of a directory of web sites in the UK, and you would be right.

Not all URLs are as meaningful, but the key point is that your browser will take you to the right site provided you type in the right address. In that respect, your browser is just like a taxi – you don't need to know where the address is or even which language it is in as long as your taxi driver

| Address | http://www.microsoft.com/insider/internet/default.htm |

(browser) does (figure 19).

Try it: after you have started Internet Explorer and the home page has loaded:

1. Click your mouse pointer in the Address box.

2. Type an address, for example: http://www.bbc.co.uk

3. Press Enter.

If the address is valid, the page will load. Depending on the speed of your Internet connection and the complexity of the web page, this could take a second or so or a few minutes. When the page has finished loading, the status bar at the bottom of the window will say Done, and the Back button on the toolbar will be available. To return to the home site, just click on the Back button. Once the home page loads, the Forward button becomes available – click on it to return to the second page (the BBC) again. You can use these two buttons to travel back to the sites you've visited.

Fig. 19. The Address Bar. Did you know that you can move your cursor into the Address bar by pressing ALT+D? You can also type a word in the Address box and press Ctrl+Enter to automatically add http://www and .com on both sides of the word.

Using AutoComplete

When you first begin using Internet Explorer 5 and visit a site where you are required to provide a user name and password, Internet Explorer displays the AutoComplete dialog box.

This dialog box prompts you to confirm whether you want Internet Explorer to remember this particular password. You can click Yes to store the password in the special list, or No to prevent Internet Explorer from storing this password.

Most likely, you clicked Yes the first time you saw this and thought that it would be useful to have Internet Explorer automatically remember your password.

▶ *Tip* – You'll notice there is a check box titled 'Don't offer to remember any more passwords.' Selecting this completely disables the Auto-Complete feature for user names and passwords on all forms. If you later want to take advantage of AutoComplete, enable the appropriate check boxes in the AutoComplete Settings dialog box.

If you do use AutoComplete, Internet Explorer will track your name, address, email address, phone numbers, and other details and fill them in whenever an online form requests the information.

Personal security issues
This feature can save time, but it can also be a security risk if someone else gets hold of your computer. To be secure, you have to disable AutoComplete: click on Tools, Internet Options, and the Content tab. Then click on the AutoComplete button and remove the check marks from the box

Fig. 20. Setting AutoComplete. You can clear any passwords or form information by clicking the applicable button on the AutoComplete settings window. Saved passwords are an invitation to others to log on to a site with your identity.

marked Forms and the one marked User Names and Passwords on Forms (figure 20).

▶ *Tip* – The AutoComplete feature is also used in the Run dialog box. When you use the Run dialog box, AutoComplete will fill in the text box with commands that you've previously used.

Also, when you type a URL into the address bar, Internet Explorer will try to guess which web site you want by comparing it with ones that you have entered before (figure 21).

AutoComplete saves URLs, passwords and form information that you have entered before. When you type information at a later date, Auto-Complete prompts you with possible matches. For example, if you regularly use a search engine, AutoComplete will remember your search words and save you having to type them in each time. These matches can include information in practically any other forms you fill in on the web.

In the Address bar, a field on a web page, or a box for a username or password, start typing the information. AutoComplete lists the possible matches as you type. If an item in the list matches what you want, click the item. If not, continue typing.

Web sites cannot access this stored information until you enter it into the form because it is encrypted on your hard drive, but other people who

Fig. 21. Internet Explorer guesses which web site you want by comparing it with ones that you have entered before.

use your computer will be able to see it if they use Internet Explorer. For example, if you have logged onto a site that needs a password, Auto-Complete may supply the password even if it is not you at the keyboard. You can change the AutoComplete settings to force Internet Explorer to save and suggest only the information you want; such as whether to use AutoComplete for web addresses, forms, and passwords, or not to use it all. You can also clear the history for any of these settings.

To adjust AutoComplete settings

1. On the Tools menu in Internet Explorer, click Internet Options.

2. Click the Content tab.

3. In the Personal information area, click AutoComplete.

4. Select the check boxes for the AutoComplete options you want to use.

▶ *Tip* – When you are typing an URL in the Address bar, AutoComplete will display its suggestion in a dropdown list. You can make this even easier by enabling the Use inline AutoComplete for web addresses setting on the Advanced tab of the Internet Options dialog box. (You will find it under the Browsing heading.) AutoComplete will then fill in the URL for you rather than making you select it from the list.

Returning to web sites that you have visited before

There are several ways of returning to web sites you have visited before. They are:

(a) the Drop Down List

(b) the Back and Forward buttons

(c) Internet Explorer Favourites

(d) the History list

Using Internet Explorer online...

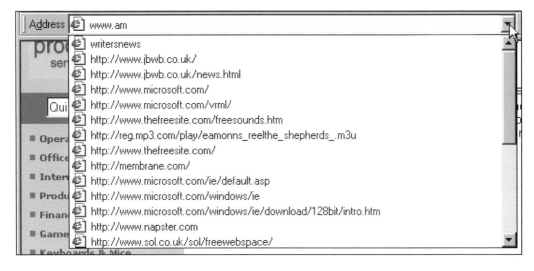

Fig. 22. The drop down list is a part of AutoComplete. The sites suggested will alter as you are typing into the address bar. If you see the address you want, click the mouse cursor on it to go to the site.

Using the Drop Down List
The drop down list (figure 22) is the simplest short cut that allows you to visit sites that you have visited before:

1. Click on the down arrow next to the drop down list to open it up. A list of recently visited sites will appear.

2. Click the URL of the site in the list that you want to revisit.

Using the Back and Forward buttons
The Back and Forward buttons (figure 23) are most useful when you want to revisit pages that you have been to in the current session.

Fig. 23. The Back button and Forward button.

Clicking on the Back button will take you to the page visited before the one presently displayed. More usefully, if you click the down arrow beside the Back button, a list of sites which you visited earlier will appear – similar to the one in the drop-down list but limited to the sites visited in one particular session. Clicking the Forward button has a similar effect but, of course, takes you forward.

▶ *Tip* – To go to the previous page, you can also press ALT+LEFT ARROW or the BACKSPACE key.

Using Internet Explorer Favorites

When you find a web site that you want to visit again, you can add its address to a list so that the next time you want to visit it, you only need to open the list and click on the entry for that site. Internet Explorer calls the list Favorites (US spelling, of course).

    To revisit a web site, just click the Favorites button on the toolbar, and then click the site title in the list.

    To add a web site to the Favorites list:

1. Go to the web site.

2. On the Favorites menu, click Add to Favorites or use the key shortcut Ctrl D.

3. Type a name for the page if you want to.

Changing the home page in your browser

If there is one particular page that you like to visit very often, you can make it your home page so that it is displayed every time you start Internet Explorer or click the Home button on the toolbar. Your home page is the page that is displayed every time you open Internet Explorer. Make sure it is a page that you want to view frequently. Or make it one that you can customise to get quick access to all the information you want, such as yahoo.com or msn.com home page. To change your home page:

1. Go to the page you want to use.

2. Open the Tools menu and click Internet Options.

3. Click the General tab.

4. In the Home page area, click Use Current.

5. To restore your original home page, click Use Default.

6. Once you've made the new setting, whenever you click the Home button in the toolbar, you'll be taken back to that page.

▶ *Tip* – You can also add a handful of sites or pages that you visit often to your Links bar.

Using the History list

If you forget to add a web site to the Favorites list or Links bar, you can click the History button on the toolbar. The History list records the sites that you have visited recently. You can change the number of days that sites are retained in the history list.

    To view your history:

1. Click the History button on your toolbar (figure 24).

Using Internet Explorer online...

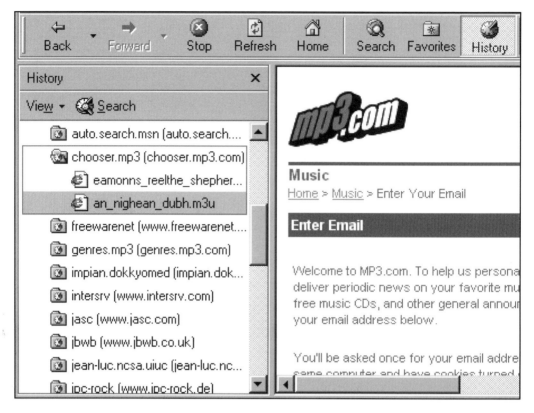

Fig. 24. The History list. Sites in your History list will often be stored in your cache so you can view them without going online again. This is useful if you want to save your phone bill and you only need to revisit the same site.

2. In the History pane on the left, click the week or day, click a web site entry to display the individual pages of that site, and then click the page title to display that page.

Internet Explorer 5 will also let you view your browsing history sorted by date, site, most-visited site, or the order visited today. Sites can be sorted by domain name, easing the task of finding the appropriate site in your History list.

To sort the History list:

1. Open a History list.

2. Click the View button (figure 25).

3. Select one of the options in the list.

4. To hide the History list, click the History button.

The History list as a security risk
The history lists may be useful but, like AutoComplete, they may also be a security risk. You may have a health problem that you want to keep private, or you may regularly visit sites that your government or company thinks are 'undesirable' or 'inappropriate'. You can manually clear the His-

Fig. 25. Clicking the View icon in order to sort a History list.

tory list on the General tab of the Internet Option dialog box. If you want to prevent Internet Explorer from creating a History list at all, set the 'Days to keep pages in history' to zero.

To change the number of days that web site addresses are retained in your history list:

1. Open the Tools menu and select Internet Options.

2. On the General tab, in the History section, set 'Days to keep pages in history' to your preferred number of days.

The cache

Quicker viewing
The content of the web pages you have already visited is stored in a special folder on your hard drive, called a cache. The idea is to help to speed up your internet viewing by keeping information that you may need again on your computer. Accessing a web page already stored on your computer is much faster than downloading it from the internet.

To see the files currently stored in your cache folder, select Tools, Internet Options, click the Settings button on the General tab, then click View Files (figure 26).

The cache size
By default, Internet Explorer allocates about 3 per cent of your hard drive space for the cache. Remember, though, that cached data occupies space on your hard disk. If you are low on disk space, you should stick with a small cache. If you have plenty of disk space to spare, there is no reason why you shouldn't use the cache to turn your computer into a virtual library of information that you have collected off the web. With a large cache, this information will be constantly available to you offline.

You are perfectly free to change the size of your cache:

1. Open the Tools menu, select Internet Options, and choose the General tab.

2. In Temporary Internet Files, click Settings. Under 'Amount of disk space to use', drag the slider to the right or left to set it according to your preferences.

Fig. 26. The cache. Setting Internet Explorer's cache size is a balance between hard disk space, privacy and usefulness. A large cache setting is the most useful because it speeds things up and saves more information locally so you don't have to connect to the internet every time you want to revisit a site.

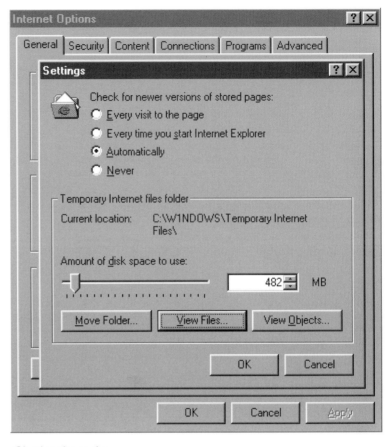

Clearing the cache
To clear your cache:

1. Open the Tools menu, select Internet Options, and choose the General tab.

2. In Temporary Internet Files, click Delete files.

3. If you surf a lot without returning to the same sites very often, it may help to purge (empty) your cache in the middle of a session. This also helps you to protect your privacy by clearing your machine of information about sites you have visited.

The way you manage your cache can be a balancing act between your requirements for privacy, convenience, and disk space.

Offline viewing

Since web pages are retrieved and stored on your computer in the cache, it should follow that you will still be able to view them after you disconnect. You can, to some extent. The browser keeps some of the pages in the cache. These pages are kept until the cache becomes full, when the older pages are automatically deleted to make room for new ones. Try it yourself with a site called All-Movie Guide ('Almost everything you need in order to find a decent film.'):

1. Go online and type in the following URL into your browser:

   http://allmovie.com

   and press Enter.

2. Wait until the page finishes loading. Then press the key shortcut Control-D to add the page to your Favorites menu in Internet Explorer.

3. Now disconnect.

To prove that offline viewing works, first make sure you are offline. Next, start your browser program but don't let it connect to the internet. Then perform the following steps:

(a) Select the File menu, then Work Offline.

(b) Open the Favorites menu.

(c) Select the All-Movie Guide entry.

(d) Watch the site load.

You do not have to disconnect each time you add a page to your favourites. Just press Control-D and move on. Offline viewing is especially useful if you want to read a page with lots of text, such as an in-depth news report or a short story. Of course, many sites such as news sources change daily or more often, and to retrieve the latest news you must connect again to refresh the site's content.

Reading bookmarked pages offline
Bookmarked pages can also be marked for offline reading and pages automatically downloaded daily, weekly, or monthly:

1. Open the Favorites menu and select Organize Favorites.

2. Click the page you want available offline.

3. Click the 'Make available offline' check box.

4. Click Properties and select the Schedule tab.

5. Click 'Using the following schedules', then the Add button.

6. Specify a suitable schedule.

7. If you want to be emailed when a site changes, select the Download tab and click: 'When this page changes, send email to' and fill in your details.

You can also make web pages available offline without adding them to your Favorites list, by saving the pages on your computer. This differs from offline viewing because the files are saved into a folder and not to the browser's cache. This way they don't expire.

Searching for sites

There are two main methods of searching for web sites: using the Address bar, and using the Search Assistant.

Using the address bar
With Internet Explorer 5, you can perform a search directly from the address bar by typing 'go', 'find', or a question mark followed by the word or phrase you want to search for. Or you can type your search phrase in the Address bar, and then click the Go button.

▶ *Tip* – you can also browse your own computer if you type the path into the Address bar. Try typing 'C:' into the address bar then press Enter.

Fig. 27. Browsing your computer. When you type the name of a folder on your computer into the address bar, Internet Explorer changes into Windows Explorer with an address bar and a links bar. Type a web address into Windows Explorer and it changes back into Internet Explorer.

When you search from the Address bar (figure 27), Internet Explorer can automatically display the web page that most likely matches what you are searching for and will list other likely sites. You can change what action Internet Explorer takes when you perform this kind of search:

1. On the Tools menu in Internet Explorer, click Internet Options.

2. Click the Advanced tab.

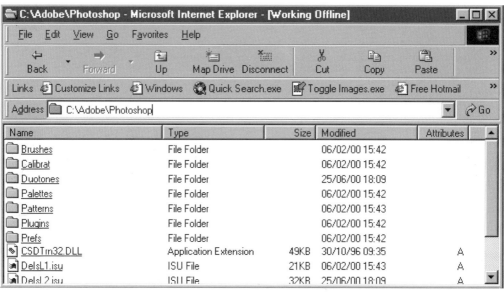

3. In the Search from the Address bar area, select the option you want.

To view a list of likely matches in the search bar with the most likely web page in the main window, select 'Display the results, and go to the most likely site'. To view a list of likely matches in the main window, select 'Just display the results in the main window'. To view only the most likely web page, select 'Just go to the most likely site'. To disable searching from the Address bar, select 'Do not search from the Address bar'.

▶ *Tip* – To quickly access the internet, create an Address toolbar on your desktop. Right-click the taskbar and select Toolbars and Address from the pop-up menu. Then, if you want, you can move the Address toolbar to the top of your desktop and configure it to Auto Hide and be Always On Top. Whenever you want to access the internet or perform a search, move your cursor to the top of the screen and the Address toolbar will appear. Use it just as you would the address bar in Internet Explorer.

Using the Search Assistant

Internet Explorer's new Search Assistant is another way in which it makes it quick and easy to find web sites. The Search Assistant offers access to several different search engines. Click the Search button and a new pane will open on the left side of your browser window (figure 28). Pick the kind of search you want to perform by clicking in the appropriate radio box. For example:

▶ web page

▶ one of your previous searches

Fig. 28. The Search Assistant. The Internet Explorer Search Assistant is an easy way to perform a quick search using UK search engines. If you want to perform a global search, however, better go direct to an international search engine such as Altavista.com.

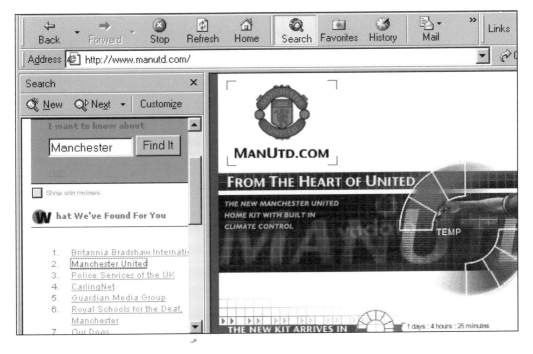

Fig. 29. Search Next.

▶ maps

▶ entertainment

▶ newsgroups

Enter the text or phrase that you want to use in your search in the search field. For example, if you want to find sites listing hotels in Southampton, you might want to enter 'Southampton hotels', then click Search. Internet Explorer 5 then uses a variety of search engines to run your search. After a few moments, you will hopefully see the results that match your search in the left pane. The most likely site will be displayed in the main window. To display one of the other sites, click its title in the left hand pane and it will open in the main window.

To run the search using a different search engine, click the Next button in the Search Assistant pane (figure 29). Internet Explorer will display the next service in the list with the search text in the search field. To start a new search, click the New button at the top of the Search Assistant pane.

To hide the search assistant again so you can view a page in a larger area, click the Search button.

Your copy of Internet Explorer may be configured to perform a search in a slightly different way to the above. But you can change the Search Assistant to suit your own preferences, see page 40.

Customising Internet Explorer

Internet Explorer may not look as you want when you first use it. You can change the appearance, the home page and many other options within Internet Explorer.

Overriding web page designs

Web page designers control the colours and size of the text on their pages, but some viewers may find the text too small or too large for comfort or the colours used may make it difficult to read. You can override the designer's settings to make the text easier to read. It's easy to customise the background and font colours to suit your own taste but you first need to set your Internet Explorer so that it will allow you to override the settings of the web pages.

1. Select Tools then Internet Options, click the General tab, and click Accessibility.

2. In the Formatting section, select the characteristics (colours, font styles and sizes) you want to be able to change and click the OK button.

3. Now you can change the appearance of web pages as you wish.

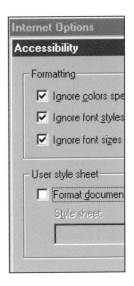

To change the size of text
1. From the menu bar, select View, Text Size.

2. The font size is usually set to Medium by default. Change it to the size you want, and the page will automatically update itself with the new size.

To change the font type
1. Open Tools then Internet Options, select the General tab and click Fonts.

2. In the dialog box that appears, select the font styles you want; then click OK twice to apply the changes.

To change background and font colours
1. Open Tools then Internet Options.

2. On the General tab, click Colours.

3. In the Colours dialog box, deselect the Use Windows Colours check box. The Text and Background options should now be available.

4. Click the boxes beside Text and Background, and select the colours you want to use from the palette. Don't select the same or similar colour for background and text because this will make it impossible to see the text.

5. In a similar way, you can also change hyperlinks from the default purple and blue and can also assign a hover colour for hyperlinks to cause them to change colours when you move your mouse over them. Click the Use Hover Colour box to put a check inside it, and then click the colour button and pick the colour from the palette.

6. Finally, click OK to apply your changes and click OK again to close the Internet Options dialog box.

Using Internet Explorer online...

To restore the defaults
You can restore the default settings at any time by selecting Tools, Internet Options, clicking Accessibility, and removing the checkmarks from the top three check boxes. Then on the General tab of the Internet Options dialog box, click Colours, and check Use Windows Colours.

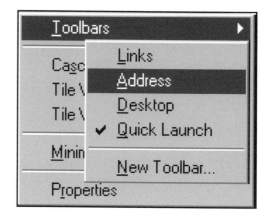

Fig. 30. Toolbars, Links, Address

Customising the toolbars
Internet Explorer 5 has four different toolbars that you can change in various ways (figure 30): the Standard Button toolbar, Links, Address, and Radio. To see which toolbars are currently visible, click on View and select Toolbars. If a toolbar has a check mark in front of it, then you should see it. To show a hidden toolbar or hide a visible one, open the View menu and then Toolbars and click on the toolbar you want to change.

▶ *Tip* – You can add or remove toolbar buttons by right-clicking the toolbar and clicking Customize. You can also resize and even reorder your buttons.

Fig. 31. Squashed up toolbars. The toolbars as they appear after being re-sized to their smallest. You can drag them down again to proper height or you can access the buttons by double-clicking the thin vertical bars to expand a single toolbar.

As you add toolbars, you will see that they stack up, sometimes so much that the web page you are viewing has only a small area left to itself. To 'squash' up the toolbars without hiding them, you can force two or more toolbars occupy the same line (figure 31). Place your mouse cursor on the bottom edge of the lower toolbar until it turns into a vertical double arrow. Now click and drag the line upwards slowly – the bottom toolbar will jump to the next line up and, if you carry on dragging upward, to the next line up until all of the toolbars are on one line with the menus. When the toolbars are combined in this way, you can slide them open by clicking and dragging or double-clicking the vertical separator.

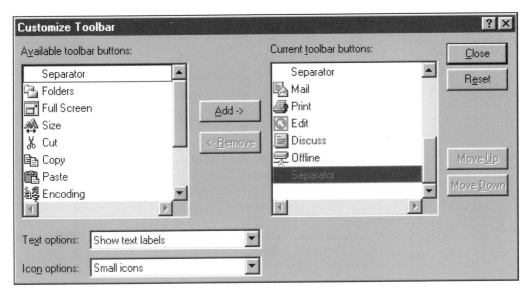

Fig. 32. Customizing the toolbars – you can add and remove buttons from the main toolbar, and change the text and icon options to streamline Internet Explorer to your tastes.

▶ *Tip* – a quick way to hide all of the toolbars in one go and view a web page full screen is to press the F11 key. To return to normal, press F11 again.

Another way of changing the appearance of the toolbars is to change the buttons on the toolbars (figure 32). You can add and remove buttons and change the size and whether they have text labels or not. To customise the buttons:

1. Right click a toolbar and select Customize to open the Customize Toolbar dialog box.

2. Select buttons to add in the left pane and click the Add button.

3. Select buttons to remove in the right pane and click the Remove button.

4. Change the text and icon options from the two drop-down lists at the bottom of the dialog box.

Some Links Bar tricks:

1. To add a shortcut, drag the web pages icon from the Address bar onto the Links bar. This also works with any link from a web page, your Favourites bar, and your desktop.

2. To remove a shortcut from the Links bar, right-click it and click Delete.

3. To rearrange shortcuts on the Links bar, simply drag them around.

4. To change a shortcuts icon, right-click it and click Properties. Click the Change Icon button.

Using Internet Explorer online...

Fig. 33. The Edit and Mail buttons.

Changing default programs

When you are using Internet Explorer 5 and you click the Edit or Mail button (figure 33), it will open certain programs to handle the appropriate tasks. Usually, the email program will be Microsoft's sister product, Outlook Express, and the editing program will be Microsoft FrontPage Express.

You can view and modify the programs currently assigned if you click on the Tools menu and select Internet Options. Then click the Programs tab. Use the pull-down menus after each category (HTML editor, email, Newsgroups and so on) to change the program associated with each function.

With Internet Explorer 5, you can choose to use a web-based email service such as HotMail or Yahoo! Mail as your default email service. When you click an email link or choose to read email or send a web page, Internet Explorer will automatically connect to your choice of web email providers.

Customising your Search Assistant

You can set up the Search Assistant so that it uses the same search engine for every search, or you can add or remove engines to the list it uses.

1. In the Search Assistant pane, click Customize. The Customize Search Settings dialog box appears.

2. To add or remove search engines, activate the Use Search Assistant For Smart Searching option, then select or deselect sites from the list that appears.

3. To use the same site for all your searches, activate the Use One Search Service For All Searches option, and then select the engine you want to use from the list.

Microsoft has improved Internet Explorer's search capabilities since Internet Explorer 4. You can now search for an email address, or street address using the Search Assistant. Internet Explorer does this in part by using AutoSearch – when you type a keyword into the URL address box, Internet Explorer will take you to the site which most closely matches that keyword. It will also open the Search pane and give you additional choices.

The Radio Toolbar

Microsoft has added a new and interesting feature to Internet Explorer 5: the Radio Toolbar (figure 34). This gives you the ability to listen to online radio stations while you are surfing the net. This feature is turned off by default.

Switching on

To turn it on permanently, go into Tools, and then into the Advanced section of Internet Options. Then, find the Multimedia section and select 'Always show Internet Explorer Radio toolbar'. Alternatively, just to view the toolbar when you need it, open the View menu and Toolbars then click on Radio.

Selecting stations

Once the Radio Bar is active, you can select one of the stations in the Radio Guide:

1. Click on the Radio Stations button, and select Radio Station Guide from the drop-down list.

2. You will see a list of radio stations.

3. Click a stations link to start playing it. It may take a few minutes for the station to load and if your internet connection is slow the music will be jerky.

4. If you don't want to use a station from the Microsoft group, use the Search Assistant and do a search using the words 'Internet radio'.

5. You can adjust the volume of the station by sliding the Volume slider, or turn the sound off temporarily by clicking the mute button (a small icon with a picture of a speaker).

The selection of stations in the Radio Station guide is fairly limited but you will come across more as you visit more sites. Interesting radio sites include:

Fig. 34. The Radio Bar – a world of audio entertainment at your fingertips.

Virgin Net live radio
http://www.virgin.net/radio/main.htm

Nexus Radio
http://www.nexus.org/Internet_Radio/

Spinner
http://www.spinner.com/

Quran
http://www.islamicdigest.org/
Readings from the Quran. The readings are in Arabic but are beautiful even to the non-Arabic speaker.

Of course, you can only listen to music if your computer is equipped with a sound card and speakers, and you'll need to have Windows Media Player installed on your machine. To see whether you have it (Windows 98), try clicking Start, Programs, Accessories and Entertainment. If you don't have Windows Media Player, you can download it from here:

Download.com
http://download.cnet.com/

Multimedia

Much of the entertainment on the internet comes in the form of multimedia such as music, video, and virtual reality. The Internet Explorer suite includes programs such as the Windows Media player, which plays music and videos, and the VRML player, which lets you explore simulated 3-dimensional worlds.

Fig. 35. The Freesite.com. Music lovers can spend hours at this site downloading new music of all kinds – from folk to punk. You can also find MIDI files – digital sound files that can be played in the background while a web page loads.

The Windows Media player will start to play automatically whenever you click on a media file or a link pointing to a media file. As it plays, Media player downloads the file. If it is a large file, such as an MP3 file, the play may well be jerky and have silent spots but once it finishes downloading, you can save it on your computer and play it from there – smoothly. To play a multimedia file on your computer, just double-click it.

▶ *Tip* – A good site for free multimedia files is TheFreeSite.com (figure 35) at:

http://www.thefreesite.com/freesounds.htm

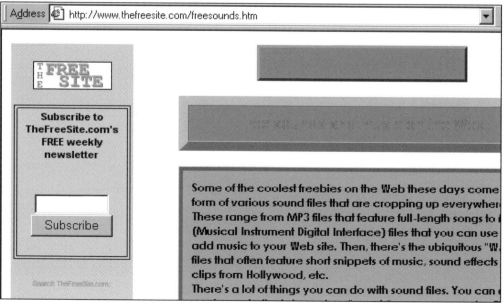

Web accessories for Internet Explorer 5

Some very useful additional features are available from Microsoft's site at

http://www.microsoft.com/Windows/IE/WebAccess/ie5tools.asp

The download comes as a file which, when you run it, will add the accessories to Internet Explorer's other features.

Most of these new features are activated by right-clicking in the browser and choosing the associated command. The added features are:

Open Frame in New Window
Often a web site will try to dominate your browsing experience by using frames. Instead of allowing you to view subsequent pages on their own, they will be presented inside frames belonging to the first site. This option will open a particular frame in a separate window. Right-click anywhere in the frame you're interested in, and select Open in New Frame.

Quick Search
This accessory, available in the links bar, further speeds up your searching by letting you use abbreviations for your favourite search sites. You can type 'av travel agents' into the address bar to start a search with AltaVista using the keywords 'travel agents'. To activate this feature, select it from the links bar and then click on the Quicksearch button.

Zoom In/Zoom Out
This feature lets you zoom into and out from images on a web page. Right-click on the image and select Zoom In or Zoom Out.

Image Toggler
Perhaps the most useful for speeding up your browsing, this feature will enable you to turn images on or off quickly. Open the Links bar and click Toggle Images.

Text Highlighter
This feature lets you highlight text in a document just like a word processor. Select your text, then right-click and choose Highlight.

Web Search
With this web accessory you can select a keyword or keywords on a web page and send them directly to a search engine to perform a search. Right-click the word of phrase, and choose Web Search.

Links List
This feature opens a new window with a list of every link on the page. Right-click anywhere on the page and select Links Lists.

Image List
This tool will list and display all the images on a web page in a separate window including the file size. The window will also calculate the download speed for all of the images. This is useful for web developers or if you just want to know how someone else has organised their images.

Others

Here are some further very popular and useful programs that you may want to download.

Adobe Acrobat Reader
http://www.adobe.com/prodindex/acrobat/main.html
Occasionally you will encounter documents which cannot be viewed by your web browser; these include PDF files – to read these documents, you need to use Acrobat Reader.

RealPlayer
http://www.realaudio.com/
With RealPlayer (figure 36) you can listen to audio files 'on demand.' The files are played while they are downloading ('streaming'), rather than waiting for the entire file to be downloaded before you can begin listening. Some radio stations work with RealAudio.

Shockwave and Flash
http://www.shockwave.com/
For viewing Macromedia Director movies and Flash files (animations). Your browser will tell you if you are viewing a page which requires the software (figure 37).

Quicktime Player
http://www.apple.com/quicktime/
Apple's software allows you to view QuickTime movies.

Fig. 36. RealPlayer is a popular tool for listening to music and audio files online.

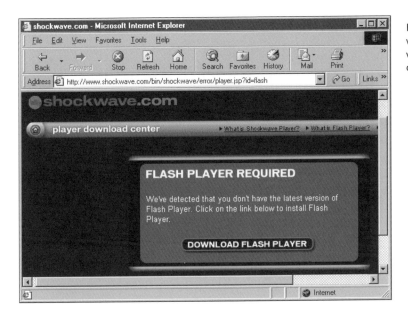

Fig. 37. Shockwave is a widely used program for viewing animation effects on web pages.

QuickTime VR
http://www.apple.com/quicktime/qtvr/
Download this player to view and explore 3D objects and places.

VDOLive
http://www.vdo.net/
This plug-in allows you to play certain real-time audio and video files.

CU-SeeMe
http://www.rocketcharged.com/cu-seeme/
CU-SeeMe is a free videoconferencing program.

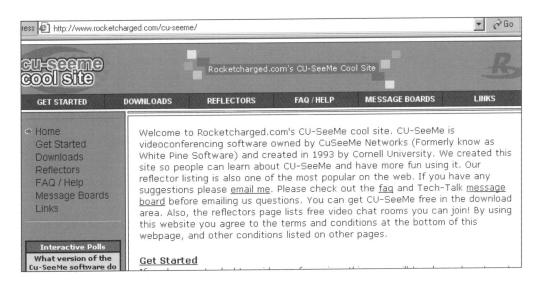

3 Using Outlook Express

In this chapter we will explore:

▶ *composing and sending a message*
▶ *connecting and disconnecting*
▶ *handling incoming messages*
▶ *using the Windows Address Book*
▶ *sending and receiving files*
▶ *virus protection*
▶ *accessing Usenet newsgroups with Outlook Express*

Fig. 38. Outlook Express is the best available email client for general use. It is easy to use and powerful; you just have to be careful of incoming emails – read the section on securing Outlook Express before you get started.

Outlook Express is an email program that comes as part of the Internet Explorer package. It is easy to use and looks good (figure 38). It also has the advantage of being able to work seamlessly with many other Microsoft programs.

Outlook Express not only lets you type in an email message but it also gives you the power to format your message in many different ways – in fact in a similar way to how you would design a web page.

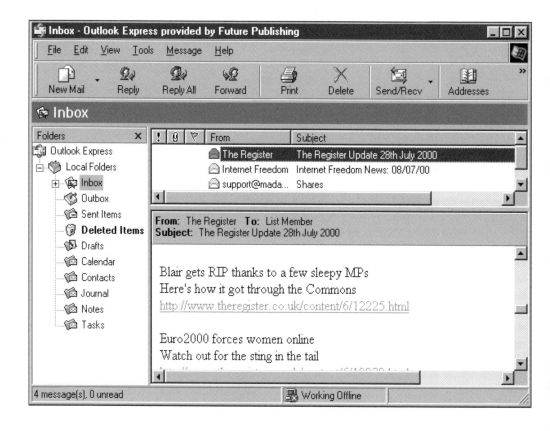

Composing and sending a message

Composing and sending an email message is easy:

1. Start Outlook Express.

2. Click New Mail (figure 39).

Fig. 39. The New Mail icon.

3. Insert the email address of the recipient.

4. Compose your message (this part can be as complicated or simple as you want!).

5. Click Send.

You can start Outlook Express in a number of ways:

(a) by clicking the Mail button in Internet Explorer

(b) by typing 'mailto:' in the Internet Explorer address bar

(c) by clicking one of the Outlook Express icons such as the one on your desktop

Composing a simple email message is done in the same way as writing a letter in a word-processing program. You can use different text styles and layouts. In addition, Outlook Express will allow you to design an email message like a web page. This means you can add images, hyperlinks and even sound clips and other multimedia components to your message. You can then save your designs as 'stationery' that you can use for future messages.

Text
In the early days, email messages were always text only – one size and no effects like bold, italics or underlining. Now, however, email clients have the power of a good word-processing program. You can change the appearance of your messages in many ways.

Email messages are formatted with hypertext markup language (HTML), the standard for formatting web pages (figure 40). With HTML, you can introduce many different kinds of fonts, text sizes and colours.

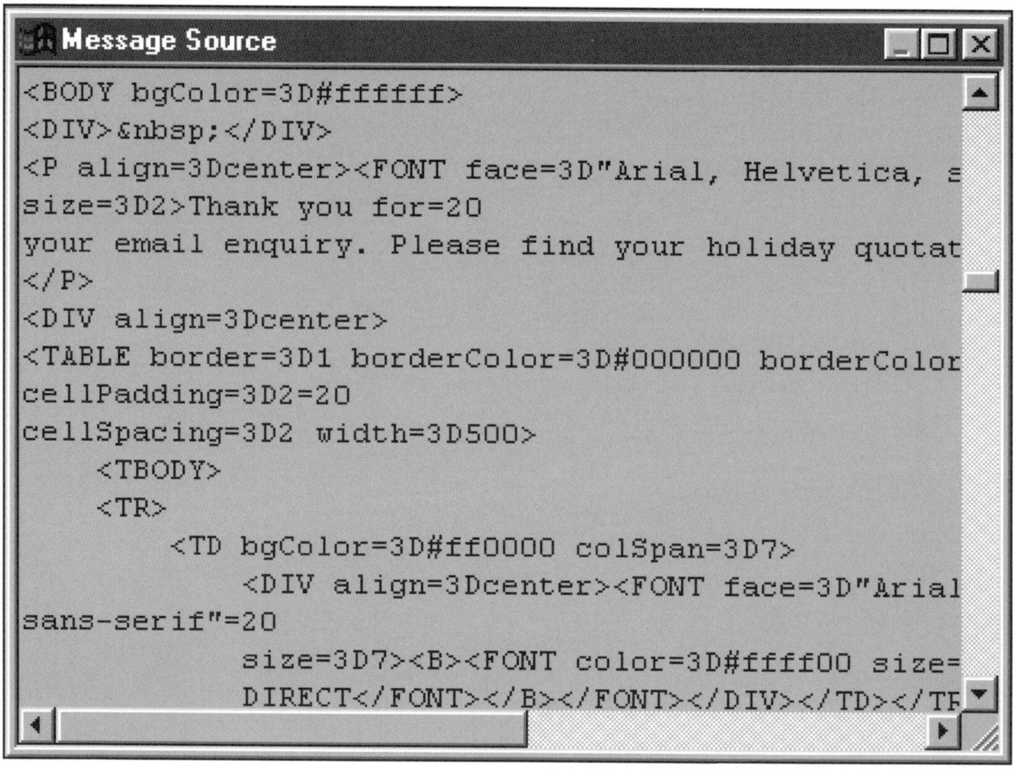

```
Message Source                                      _ □ ✕

<BODY bgColor=3D#ffffff>
<DIV> </DIV>
<P align=3Dcenter><FONT face=3D"Arial, Helvetica, s
size=3D2>Thank you for=20
your email enquiry. Please find your holiday quotat
</P>
<DIV align=3Dcenter>
<TABLE border=3D1 borderColor=3D#000000 borderColor
cellPadding=3D2=20
cellSpacing=3D2 width=3D500>
    <TBODY>
    <TR>
        <TD bgColor=3D#ff0000 colSpan=3D7>
            <DIV align=3Dcenter><FONT face=3D"Arial
sans-serif"=20
            size=3D7><B><FONT color=3D#ffff00 size=
            DIRECT</FONT></B></FONT></DIV></TD></TF
◀                                               ▶
```

Fig. 40. HTML in an email message. You can view the normally hidden HTML coding of an email message. Just right-click the message in the inbox, select Properties, click the Details tab, and click the Message Source button. Viewing the message in this way shows you how much space HTML can really add to a message.

This is how to use HTML formatting on an individual message with Outlook Express:

1. Start a new email message.

2. Make sure that HTML formatting is turned on by opening the Format menu. If the black dot appears by Rich Text (HTML), then HTML formatting is turned on.

To use HTML formatting on all outgoing messages with Outlook Express:

(a) Open the Tools menu, click Options, and then the Send tab.

(b) In the Mail Sending Format, click HTML.

You can change the look of all your messages or you can make changes to selected text within a single message.
    To change the text style in all messages:

1. In the Tools menu, click Options.

2. Click the Compose tab, and then click the Font Settings button.

To format text within individual messages:

3. Select the text you want to change.

4. Use the formatting toolbar to create the effect you want.

When you start a new message thereafter, you will be able to format it using HTML. Select the text and use the Format menu to change the appearance of your text.

Pictures
With HTML formatting you can also add graphics to your messages. To insert a picture:

(a) Click the point in the message where you want the image to appear.

(b) Open the Insert menu, click Picture, and then click Browse to find your image file.

(c) Change the layout and spacing or the image.

If the Picture command is not available, turn on HTML formatting by opening the Format menu and then clicking Rich Text (HTML). A black dot should be visible next to the command.

To set a picture to be used as a background for a message, click the Format menu, select Background, then Picture. Click the Browse button to search for the image you want to use.

Adding multimedia to your message
It is easy to include a sound in a message so that as soon as someone views your message, it will play the sound. To insert a sound in your message:

1. Click anywhere in the message window.

2. Open the Format menu, click Background, then Sound (figure 41).

3. Enter the name of the file you want to include and the number of times you want the file to play.

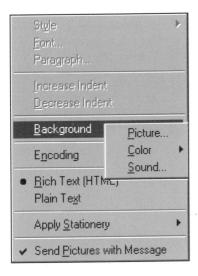

Fig. 41. Adding a picture, colour or sound to the background of a web page.

49

You will find some sound files in the Windows\media folder if you want to try it out.

More HTML
A further step is to use a web page that has already been created and use it as a template with which you can compose your own messages.

▶ *Example* – Say you have designed or seen a site that uses a certain combination of font, background image, and overall design that you really like. You can tell Outlook Express to open that page for you to use and then change the layout and content of the design so it suits your purposes. You can replace the content of the page with your own message and pictures then tweak any other features that you want to change.

There are some things to be aware of when sending messages designed in this way, though.

(a) If you use somebody else's design without changing it enough, you may be liable to some kind of copyright violation.

(b) The size of the message may increase so much that it takes a long time for you to send it.

(c) More importantly, the recipient will have to take more time download-ing the message – thus increasing their telephone bill.

However, if you still want to try:

1. Open the Message menu.

2. Choose 'New message using'

3. Select Web page.

4. Enter the address of the web page you want to use.

Connecting and disconnecting

Although designing and writing your email messages can take a long time, especially if you are a creative person, you don't have to be con-nected to the internet to compose your messages. You only need connect when you want to send and receive your messages.

▶ *Tip* – If you do not want to connect to the internet, clicking the Send button puts your messages in your Outbox until you do want to send them.

If you are connected to the internet, the message will be sent as soon as you press the Send button.
  Once you are connected to the internet, starting Outlook Express will

Fig. 42. Click this button if you want to send or receive messages.

send any mail from your Outbox and collect any incoming email that is waiting for you. In fact, you can also set it to up to check for new emails periodically while you are online doing other things, say browsing the web.

If Outlook Express is already running when you connect, click the Send/Recv button (figure 42) to send any messages that have been placed in the Outbox. Any incoming messages will also be retrieved and will appear in your Inbox.

You can also save on your telephone bill if you disconnect from the internet as soon as all your new messages, if you have any, have been retrieved. You can then read them at leisure when offline.

Handling incoming messages

To read a message, simply find it in your Inbox then double-click on it in the right-hand pane. Single-clicking will also work, but you will see the contents of the message in the preview pane or your email client instead of in a separate window.

If you are unsure how to find your Inbox folder:

1. Open the View menu.

2. Click Go to folder.

3. Select Inbox.

4. Click OK.

Replying to a message
Replying to a message is easy. Open the message and click on the Reply button. When you reply to a message, Outlook Express will automatically fill in the email address. It will also include the content of the original message in the body of the reply.

Forwarding a message
Forwarding a message is almost identical to replying to one except you send it to a person other than the one who sent it. You might want to forward a joke on to another of your friends for example.

When you reply to a message, your email client automatically fills in the email address of the person who sent it; when you forward a message, you must supply the email address of the recipient yourself, either by using the Windows Address Book or by typing it in.

To forward a message:

1. Select the message you want to forward.

2. Click the Forward button.

3. Fill in the address of the recipient.

4. Add your comments.

5. Click Send.

The contents of the original message are included in the message similar to when you reply to someone – you can also, of course, add your own message or comments to the message.

Sending a message to more than one person
When you send an email message to someone, you put their email address in the 'To:' section. If you want to send the same message to other people, include their addresses in the 'Cc:' section. Cc stands for carbon copy – a term that comes from the office environment where sending copies of business letters to other interested parties is usual practice.

'Cc:' is useful if you want to notify a number of people of an event. You can send, for example, a wedding invitation to all of your friends and family by writing one message: address it to one person and put the addresses of all of the other people in the 'Cc:' section. That way, everyone receives the same message and everyone will be able to see who else has been invited.

What if there was someone whose email address you did not want to appear in the list? Say you have a surprise guest, you can hide that persons address by putting it in the 'Bcc:' (blind carbon copy) section. Any email addresses in the Bcc section will be invisible to other recipients of the message.

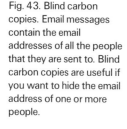
Fig. 43. Blind carbon copies. Email messages contain the email addresses of all the people that they are sent to. Blind carbon copies are useful if you want to hide the email address of one or more people.

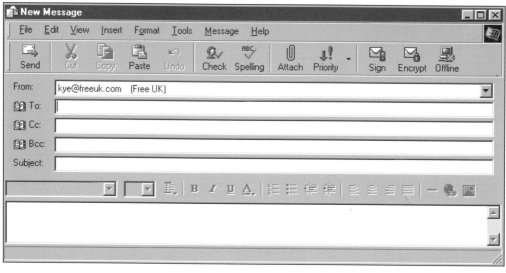

To enter an address in the 'Bcc:' section:

1. Start a new message.

2. Fill in the other recipients of the message in the 'To:' and 'Cc:' sections.

3. Open the View menu.

4. Select View all Headers to show the 'Bcc:' section.

5. Fill in the address of the invisible recipient.

Once you have filled in the addresses, compose your message as normal and click Send.

Managing your incoming email
After a while, a number of email messages will start to accumulate in your Inbox. Most email clients will allow you to manage your email both manually and automatically. You can delete, copy, move, and filter messages in many different ways.

Deleting
Deleting messages is the easiest way to tidy up your Inbox. It is only a simple click away: select the messages you wish to delete and click the Delete button (figure 44).

Fig. 44. The delete button.

After you delete a message, however, it is not lost. The 'deleted' message is just transferred to the Deleted Items folder. It is kept there until you delete it permanently. You can also set Outlook Express to empty the folder on exit if you open the Tools menu and select Options. Click on the Maintenance tab, and tick the box next to Empty messages from the deleted folder on exit.

Moving and filtering incoming messages
As well as deleting messages, you can create new folders. You can then have Outlook Express automatically move incoming messages into those folders according to the type of messages they are. For example, you might want a message folder specifically for your family and friends. You might want another one for regular newsletters, and another for business emails.
To create a new folder:

1. Select your Inbox in the folders pane.

2. Click on File, then New, and select Folder....

3. Give the new folder a name.

You can manually move messages around or copy them, but it saves time if you set up filters to do this for you. The criteria you decide to use to filter messages can be any part of the incoming messages or articles:

(a) Who the message is to.

(b) Who it is from.

(c) What the subject contains.

(d) What the body text contains.

Fig. 45. Outlook Express filters. Set filters so that mail originating from known sources (friends, mailing lists, etc.) is moved to separate folders; this means that anything appearing in your in tray is from an unknown source and is immediately visible.

Outlook Express can scan incoming emails and move them to different directories according to any of the above. It can also perform many other tasks automatically such as copying, deleting, replying with another message, forwarding to someone, marking, and so on.

You can also set multiple filters to look at different parts of an incoming message and perform a variety of tasks depending on what it finds (figure 45). For example, if you receive a message from a mailing list, you could have the email program automatically move it to a special folder and if it is

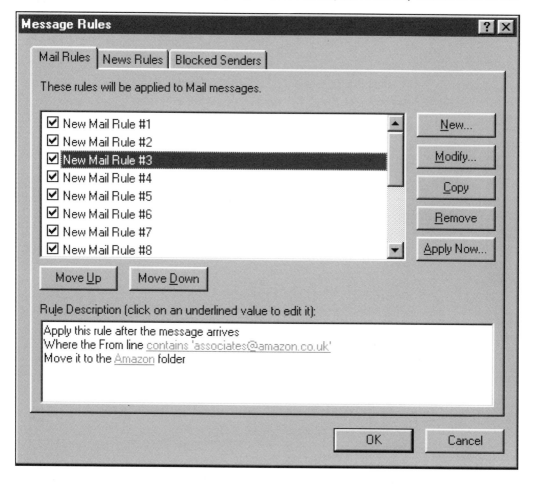

from a certain person on that list, it could then mark it in colour to make you aware of it.

Combining different rules
You can combine rules in many ways such as:

1. Where the From line contains Kye Valongo

2. and the Subject line contains Internet Handbooks,

3. highlight the message in red

4. and move it to the Work folder.

Applying rules to your messages
You can use rules to mark certain messages, highlight messages in colour, have certain messages downloaded, or even delete unwanted messages before you see them.
    This is how to create a rule (figure 46):

1. Open the Tools menu and select Message Rules.

2. Click Mail. On the Mail Rules tab, click New.

3. Select the conditions for your rule by checking or clearing the check boxes in the Conditions section – for example Where the From line contains people.

4. You can also specify multiple conditions for a single rule by clicking more than one check box.

5. Click the hyperlinks (in this case, the underlined text: contains people) in the Rule Description section to fill in the details of your rule (in this case, to select a person).

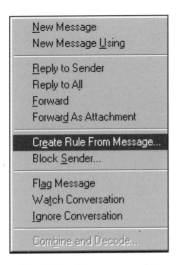

Fig. 46. Creating message rules.

6. If you have more than one condition, you can also determine whether all of the rule conditions must be met (and) or whether at least one must be met (or).

7. In the Name of the rule box, type a new name for your rule, and then click OK.

8. The next time you receive messages, these filters will take effect.

Coping with junk email

If you are new to the internet your mailbox will be fairly quiet. But, rest assured, once you have been around for a while, you will be seen as fair game for the many junk mailers on the internet. Junk email is often called spam – from a Monty Python sketch. Spam usually has an absurd title that gives it away such as:

!!!!Earn thousands in no time!!!!

Fig. 47. Net Services. Spam or unsolicited mail is worse than the junk you receive through your letterbox – you pay to receive email junk.

Filters are particularly useful for combating spam (figure 47). You might want to filter all of your usual email messages into their own classified folders such as family, friends, work, and news. Any messages that remain in your Inbox are then likely to be junk mail of some kind. You will thus quickly be able to see when you get a message that you want to read because it will appear in one of the other folders. If you repeatedly receive junk from the same person, you can also set up a filter to delete the message before you even read it.

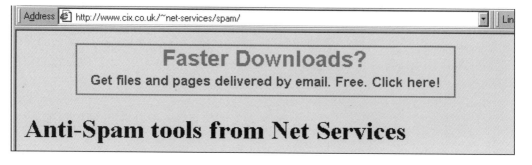

Using the Windows Address Book

Email addresses are very difficult to remember. But, just as you would keep the addresses of your friends and colleagues in an address book, so you can also keep the email addresses of your internet contacts in the address book that is part of your email client (figure 48). They store email addresses and many other details such as names, addresses, phone numbers, website addresses, fax numbers, job descriptions and other information.

Outlook Express shares the Windows address book which usually comes installed on all Windows PCs.

Adding entries to your address book
To add an entry to your address book:

1. Open theTools menu in Outlook Express.

2. Select Address Book. (You can also open the address book by clicking theAddresses button on the main toolbar.)

3. Open the File menu.

4. Select New, then New Contact.

5. Fill in the details you want to store in the address book, including the email address.

Sending an email message using the address book
Once you have someone's email address in the address book, you will be able to send that person a message with a couple of mouse clicks instead of having to laboriously type in their email address by hand. All you need to do is open the address book, find the person's entry and click on the command for a new message.
In Outlook Express:

▶ Open theTools menu.

▶ Select Address book.

▶ Right click over the person's entry.

Fig. 48.TheWindows address book allows you to record much more than just a person's email address – such as their address, telephone number and more.

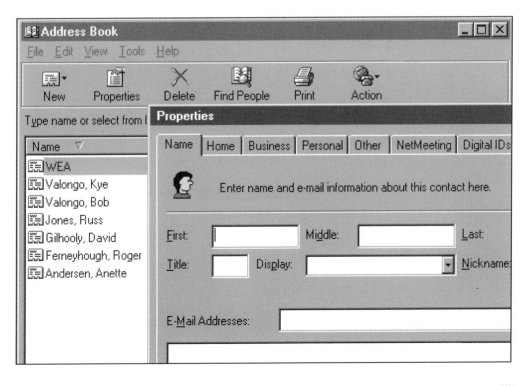

Using Outlook Express ....

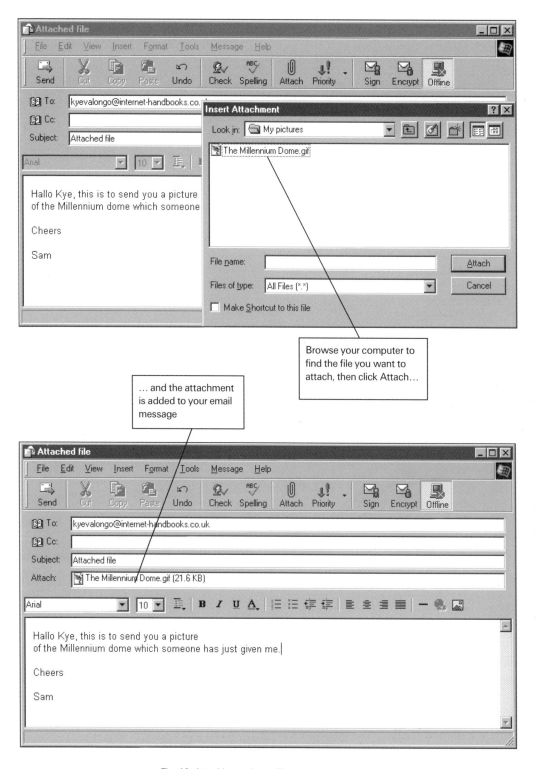

Fig. 49. Attaching a picture file to an email message.

▶ Select Action then Send mail.

Sending and receiving files

Attachments
There is much more to email than just sending text messages. For example, you can easily send pictures, video clips and other files attached to email messages. This could be a wedding photograph or a financial spreadsheet.

To attach a file to an email message, all you need to do is to start a new message. Then, click the Attach button and select the file you wish to send (figure 49).

Attaching large files
Some files, such as scanned photos, can be very large and will take a long time to send. This may increase your (and the recipient's) telephone costs. Scanned images, for example, can be especially large and can easily take over an hour to send.

Virus protection

Sending and receiving files by email always carries the risk of computer viruses. Once your computer is infected, a virus will automatically reproduce and infect other programs.

▶ *Virus* – A small program that can reproduce itself and cause damage to equipment and data stored on computer systems. All computer viruses are devised by human beings. Even a simple virus can cause irreparable damage.

Viruses can be as harmless as displaying a message on your screen. They can also be dangerous enough to completely corrupt your hard drive. Viruses will also spread themselves by email to other people whose addresses are in your Windows Address Book. If you insert disks into your computer, receive email messages, share disks, or download files from the internet, you are likely to encounter viruses.

Protecting against virus infection
The number one precaution you should take right now is to get some virus scanning software. And once you have some, make sure you update it frequently: new viruses appear every day. The following precautions are simple but very effective:

1. Never start by opening a downloaded or attached file. Save it first.

2. Scan the file with an up-to-date virus scanner before running or opening it. It may help to create a special quarantine directory or folder on your hard drive for this purpose.

3. You may have changed your browser's settings, so it can automatically open downloaded files. If so, disable it now. It may be a little inconvenient but it could save you hours of work.

4. Back up your files regularly. Keep all the backup disks or tapes in a safe place.

Antivirus software
Since new viruses appear frequently, you should get antivirus software that promises regular and frequent updates. Any good antivirus software should:

(a) be up to date – you should obtain updates as soon as one is available.

(b) conform to standards set by the National Computer Security Association.

(c) be able to scan floppy disks, hard drives, CD-ROMs, and network drives.

(d) be able to monitor your computer while you are working, so it can warn you if you try to open an infected file.

(e) include a version of the scanner that can be run on a bootable floppy disk.

F-Prot
http://www.isvr.soton.ac.uk/ftp/pc/f-prot
One of the best scanners is F-Prot, from Iceland and is available at the above address. F-Prot is free for private use (figure 50).

Download.com
http://www.download.com
At this well-known web site you can download other free antivirus software. For example you can obtain Disinfectant for Macintosh and trial versions of other commercial antivirus software. Perhaps the most

Fig. 50. F-Prot is a good source of anti-virus software.

important thing you need to do is read the instructions that come with the antivirus software and follow them strictly. Some of the well-known brands of antivirus software include Dr Solomon from Symantec, and McAfee.

Macro viruses
Most documents can now contain computer programs called macros within them. For example, you can have a word processor document that automatically performs some task when it is opened. Virus writers have taken advantage of this and have written macro viruses that infect, say, Microsoft Word and Excel documents. For more information see:

http://www.microsoft.com/security

Accessing Usenet newsgroups with Outlook Express

Newsgroups
Usenet is like Hyde Park Corner on the internet. It is a vast virtual meeting place where people all over the world can discuss events and keep up with news. In fact, people talk about absolutely anything that interests them. These discussions are segregated into topics within separate forums called newsgroups.

There are over 80,000 newsgroups in Usenet. Almost every hobby or interest you can imagine has one or more newsgroups dedicated to it.

Articles and threads
A message in a newsgroup is a kind of public email, but the messages are handled by Outlook Express in a particular way. Messages in newsgroups are called articles. They are grouped or batched together according to the topic discussed. A batch of articles which has stemmed from one particular article is called a thread. You can see the progress of a particular discussion (threaded discussion) as one person after another replies to the original message. These news articles are stored on your ISP's computer, or news server.

Newsgroup hierarchies and names
The names of the newsgroups often seem arbitrary and meaningless to outsiders. However, they do describe to some extent what kind of topic the group was created for. Newsgroup names are abbreviated descriptions of the topic of interest. They consist of a hierarchy of sections separated by dots. There is, for example, a newsgroup dedicated to the BBC series *Eastenders* (figure 51) called:

rec.arts.tv.uk.eastenders

There is another one for football enthusiasts called:

uk.sport.football

The rec. part of rec.arts.tv.uk.eastenders and the uk part of uk.sport.football are the top-level hierarchies of the newsgroups. The uk part means that the group concerns a UK-related topic. The rec one implies a topic to

Using Outlook Express ....

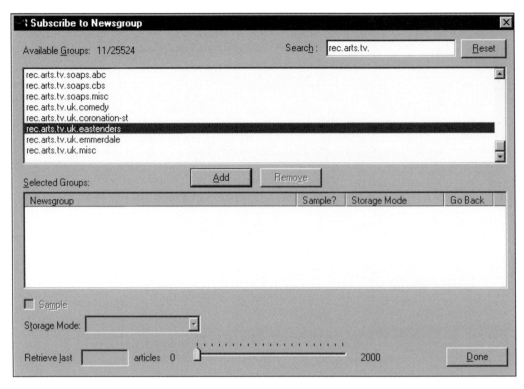

Fig. 51. There is even a
newsgroup for the BBC
series *Eastenders*.

do with recreation. Another top-level hierarchy is comp which contains
groups discussing computer-related topics.

These broad top-level areas are followed by more specific topics such
as arts (for art-related topics), sport (for sport subjects), and periphs (for
peripherals). So comp.periphs is limited to discussions about computer
peripherals (printers, scanners, mice etc.) and at a lower level again, discussions in the group comp.periphs.printers are limited to only those
about printers.

Getting ready to join newsgroups
Before you can start taking part in newsgroup discussions, you must
follow some simple steps:

1. Configure (set up) and connect to a news server.

2. Download a large list of thousands of newsgroups supplied by that
    news server.

3. Subscribe to the individual newsgroups that interest you.

4. Download batches of messages from those individual newsgroups.

Configuring or adding a news server
Most ISPs will configure (set up) Outlook Express and Internet Explorer
automatically, but you can do it yourself fairly easily. There is a wizard that
steps you through the process (figure 52).

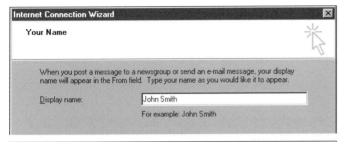

Fig. 52(a). Setting up your news server. First enter your user name.

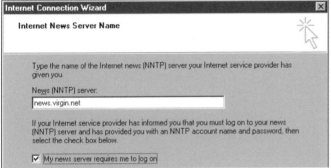

Fig. 52(b). Enter the name of the news server you want to use (in the example it is news.virgin.net).

Fig. 52(c). Enter your full email address.

Fig. 52(d). *Below*: When you log on to the internet, Outlook Express will contact your news server and display a long A-Z list of thousands of newsgroups.

63

(a) Select the Tools menu, then Accounts, then click on the Add button.

(b) Select News. Outlook Express will now start the internet connection wizard.

(c) Select the name and email address you wish to use in any articles you send.

(d) Finally, enter the name of your ISP's news server. For example, in figure 53 the name of the news server is FreeNet.

Fig. 53. The news server Properties window shows which news server is already available to the computer user (in this case FreeNet), and gives the opportunity to change it or add new ones.

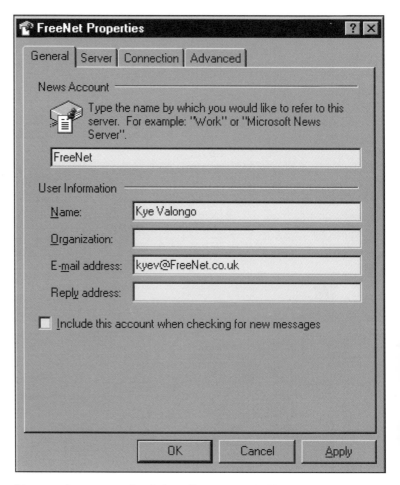

You can change your details later if you open the Tools menu and select Accounts. Select the News tab, then double click on the news server. In this Properties window, you can change server address or any of the other details such as your email address or name.

Subscribing to newsgroups
The first time you want to explore Usenet, you must download a list of newsgroups:

1. Click on the news server in the Folders frame. For example, if you are a customer of Virgin, the name will be: news.virgin.net

2. When you highlight the news server, Outlook Express will ask you if you want to view a list of available newsgroups. Select Yes. Outlook will then try to connect to the news server and download the list.

Once you have the list of newsgroups, subscribing to one or more is easy:

(a) Highlight the news server in the Folders frame and click the News-groups button in the preview pane.

(b) Select the newsgroup you are interested in.

(c) Click Subscribe.

Finding the newsgroups you want
You may have trouble wading through the thousands of newsgroups to find the one or ones you want. If so, you can easily search for a news-group name by entering your keywords in the box underneath 'Display newsgroups which contain'

► *Example* – If you are interested in classical guitars and you know the name of the relevant group, you would enter rec.music.classical. guitar or, if you are unsure of the name of the group, you can just enter guitar. Entering guitar brings up a list of about twenty different groups with the text guitar as part of the name. Highlight the group you want to subscribe to and click the Subscribe button. Click OK. You will see the group name appear in the Folder window underneath the server name. You can also double-click a name in the Newsgroup list to subscribe. If you now click the Goto button, you will be con-nected to the internet and Outlook Express will download articles from that newsgroup.

Display newsgroups which

music

Newsgroup

alt.music.311
alt.music.4-track
alt.music.4ad
alt.music.a-cappel
alt.music.a-perfec
alt.music.abba
alt.music.acid-jazz
alt.music.adiemus
alt.music.aerosmitl
alt.music.african

Quitting a newsgroup
You can easily cancel your subscription to a newsgroup at any time:

1. Click the Newsgroups button, then the Subscribed tab.

2. Select the group, and then click the Unsubscribe button.

You can also right-click the newsgroup in the Folders list and then click Unsubscribe.

Downloading and reading articles

To download articles from the newsgroup, connect to the internet and just click on the newsgroup name in the Folders window (figure 54). Outlook will then download any new articles from the news server and they will appear in the preview pane.

Using Outlook Express ....

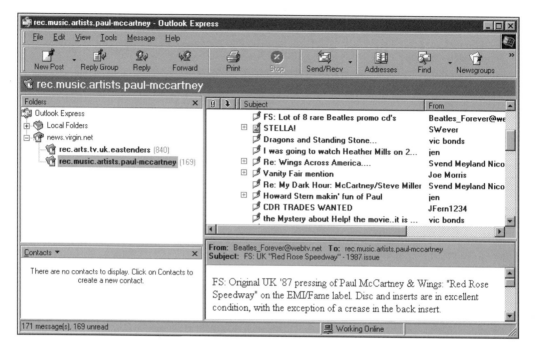

Fig. 54. Using Outlook Express for newsgroups. In the left pane, the name of a newsgroup is highlighted. The message headers then appear in the top right pane. Click on any message header to view the full message in the lower right pane.

Outlook Express also has a synchronise feature whereby it downloads the articles and subject lines from all of your subscribed groups in one go. Usually, Outlook Express will only download the subject line (which it calls headers) but you can configure it to download the whole body of the article when you select the group:

(a) Select the newsgroup.

(b) Open the File menu, and select Properties.

(c) Click the Synchronise tab and check When synchronising this newsgroup, download: and select one of: New headers, New messages (Headers and bodies), or All messages (Headers and bodies).

(d) Now click OK, and then click the Synchronise button.

Posting and replying to newsgroup messages
There are several ways in which you can post messages, depending on whether you are posting a new message or replying to one. In the Folders list, select the newsgroup you want to post a message to.

To post a new article, click the New Post button. Enter the Subject of your article, write the message you want to send and then click the Send button.

Cross-posting
It is possible to cross-post your message, in other words send it to multiple newsgroups all at the same time. Click the icon next to Newsgroups in

the New Message dialog box before you click the Send button. In the Pick Newsgroups dialog box, select the newsgroups from the list, and then click Add.

Remember, though, if you continually send the same message to many newsgroups, people may get sufficiently irritated to complain to your ISP, which in turn could even lead to your account being terminated. It is sensible to cross-post to no more than about three or four groups.

Cancelling a message
To cancel a message you have posted select the message once it has appeared in the newsgroup, click the Message menu, and then select Cancel Message.

More Internet Handbooks to help you

Discussion Forms on the Internet: A practical step-by-step guide to news-groups, mailing lists and bulletin board services, Kye Valongo (Internet Handbooks).

Using Email on the Internet: A step-by-step guide to sending and receiving messages and files, Kye Valongo (Internet Handbooks).

Visit the free Internet HelpZone at
www.internet-handbooks.co.uk
Helping you master the internet

---

4 Using FrontPage Express

In this chapter we will explore:

▶ *using wizards*
▶ *working with text*
▶ *adding pictures to your web page*
▶ *using tables in a web page*
▶ *adding some links to a web page*

To make your own web site, you need a program for designing the individual pages. FrontPage Express comes with Internet Explorer and is a very powerful web editor (figure 55). In fact, it may be all you ever need to create and maintain your own site.

This section provides information to help you to create a simple web page with Microsoft Frontpage Express. Most of the methods covered here will also work with the full version of Frontpage.

▶ *HTML* – Hypertext markup language. The formatting of a web page is accomplished by hidden codes within the page. You normally only see the codes if you are editing a page. When you view a page normally, you see the effects of the codes.

Fig. 55. FrontPage Express is a very powerful web page editor.

FrontPage Express allows you to create your own web sites easily without needing to know any HTML. You can use FrontPage Express to create

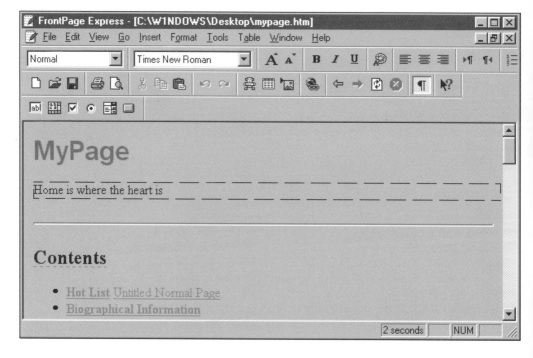

and format web pages in a WYSIWYG view: 'What you see is what you get'. This means that you can see your formatting as it would appear on the published web page.

As a simple example, bold text might appear on a web site as:

Free Music!

If you edited the page, or if you used Notepad to view the page, though, you would see:

< BOLD > Free Music! < /BOLD >

The text is surroundeded by special codes, called tags, contained inside angle brackets. These tell the viewer's browser to change the text to bold. This is the essence of web site formatting – the formatting is done on the viewer's computer by a web browser. The web page itself carries the simple text plus the HTML codes.

No need for HTML!
FrontPage Express allows you to create web pages without having to use the HTML directly. In the example above, you would simply select the text 'Free Music!' and click the Bold button. FrontPage Express inserts the HTML to embolden the text automatically. If you are used to using a word processor, you will have most of the experience you need to use FrontPage Express effectively. The formatting toolbar is very similar (figure 56).

Fig. 56. A formatting toolbar. You can use this to create text effects such as heading sizes, font styles and sizes, bold, italic, and underlining, and alignment of text (left, right or centred).

Templates and wizards
FrontPage Express comes with a range of templates and wizards which make the task even easier. A template is simply a document that has been made already – all you have to do is change the text and pictures to your own. A wizard is similar but in certain stages of the design process it asks you questions about the content of the page and gives you choices on the format of the page.

Using wizards

A wizard will guide you through, for example, the steps in creating a home page. During the process it will ask you to supply your email address, telephone number and other information you would like to appear on the page.

You will also be asked which type of web page you want to make. You could tell the wizard to make you a personal home page, or a survey form, for example, and to include your work phone number on the page. These helpful wizards cut out a lot of the work associated with creating a web page from scratch.

Using FrontPage Express...

Probably the best way to learn how to use FrontPage Express is to jump in at the deep end and create a web page for yourself using the wizards – and the water is not really very deep.

Practice example
Try creating this simple home page:

(a) Start FrontPage Express and Open the File menu.

(b) Click New.

(c) Select the Personal Home Page Wizard from the list.

(d) Click OK.

The wizard (figure 57) will start and ask you what major sections you would like to include on your page. For this example, select the following:

Hot list: interesting web sites

Biographical information

Personal interests

Contact information

Fig. 57. The Personal Home Page Wizard in FrontPage Express will make things easy for you.

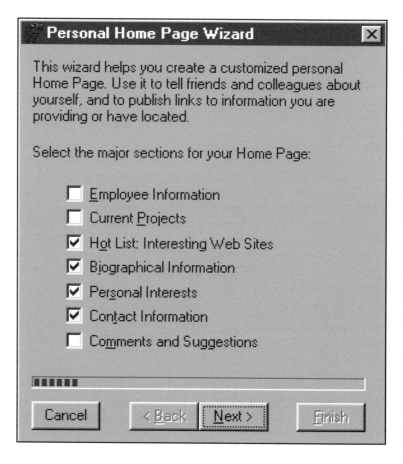

Personal Home Page Wizard ☒

This wizard helps you create a customized personal Home Page. Use it to tell friends and colleagues about yourself, and to publish links to information you are providing or have located.

Select the major sections for your Home Page:

☐ Employee Information
☐ Current Projects
☑ Hot List: Interesting Web Sites
☑ Biographical Information
☑ Personal Interests
☑ Contact Information
☐ Comments and Suggestions

| Cancel | < Back | Next > | Finish |

Deselect any other options in the list, then click Next. You will be asked the page URL and Title.

1. Enter mypage.htm for the URL. Enter MyPage as the page title. Click Next.

2. You will be asked how you want your hot list to be formatted. Select Bulleted list. Click Next.

3. Select a style for your biography. Choose Personal. Click Next.

4. You will be asked for some items for your biography section, pressing the enter key after each line and then select Definition list. You could enter a list of your hobbies.

5. Remember to press the Enter key after each hobby. Click Next when you are finished.

6. Tick the contact information to include on your home page: postal address and email address for this example, then enter the information on the right hand side. Click Next.

7. The next step allows you to change the order of the sections in your home page. If you select any item in the list, you can then move it up or down as you please. Leave them as they are for the moment and click Next.

8. Click Finish.

The basic home page
You should now be looking at the basic home page. The basic information and sections should appear in the places that you specified during the wizard questions. The wizard has placed a contents list just below the title area with links to the other sections on the page. Further down, you will see the other sections that the wizard has added for you containing some of the information that you gave it.

Now you have the page like this, you can alter any aspect of it, deleting, adding and changing items as you wish. As you can see, the page at the moment is quite plain. There is still plenty you can do to make your site more attractive, though. Before you go any further, save the page on your computer.

Saving your new home page
To save the page:

(a) Open the File menu and select Save.

(b) Click the As File button.

(c) Name the file mypage.htm, choose a directory to save it into, and then click the Save button.

Using FrontPage Express..

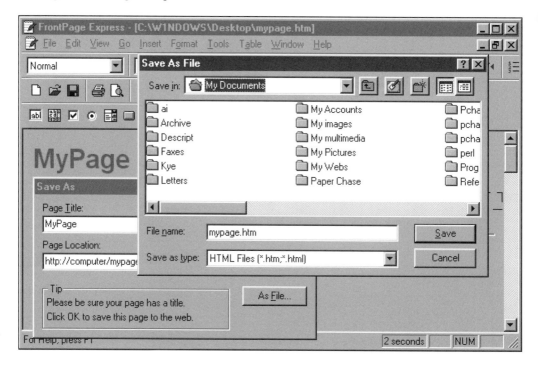

Fig. 58. Saving a web page in FrontPage Express.

(d) To view your new page as it would appear on the web, just double-click on the file mypage.htm and Internet Explorer will start (figure 58).

Using templates

A template is a pre-designed page that will serve a particular purpose in your web site. FrontPage Express comes with some templates which you can use to begin creating your own pages. Of the templates available, the Normal Page is the only one that will be practical for a home page. The other two templates usually mean that you will have to make special arrangements with your ISP before you can use them. For more information on what you can do with your web space, consult your ISP's help pages.

Working with text

As mentioned above, designing a web page with FrontPage Express is very similar to writing a letter in a word processor. You will probably recognise many of the controls and buttons on the various toolbars and menus.

Add a subheading to your page: click your mouse cursor on the title, go to the end of the line and press Enter to create a new line underneath the title. Type:

Welcome to my home page

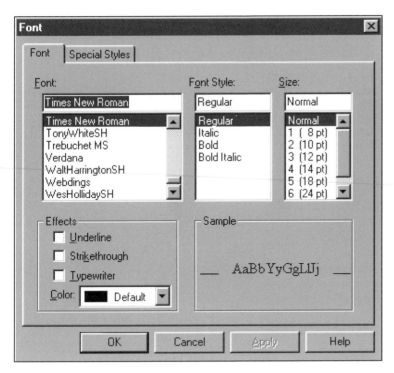

Fig. 59. Choosing a font, font style, and font size. A sample of what the text will then look like is shown lower right.

You will notice that the text style has automatically been changed to 'Normal' and is smaller than the title's font.

Making the text look the way you want
You can change the font face, style, size, and colour of text at any time.

1. Select the text and right-click. Now click Font Properties on the short-cut menu.

2. On the Font tab (figure 59), select a Font, Font Style, Size, and text Colour that you like.

You can also select one or more options under 'Effects'. You can see how the text will look in the preview area. Try experimenting with the text you have just typed.

To change the alignment and to set bold, underlined or italic text, use the buttons on the Format toolbar (figure 60).

Fig. 60. Selecting a toolbar to format your text.

▶ *Tip* – You can show or hide FrontPage Express toolbars in a similar way to how you would in Internet Explorer: open the View menu and select the toolbars you want visible.

The scrolling marquee

Add a final touch by adding a scrolling marquee – i.e. text that will move across the page. The effect is rather like you see in those scrolling advertisements on big city centre buildings:

1. Create a new line underneath the subheading.

2. Select the Insert menu, then Marquee.

3. Type 'Home is where the heart is' into the Text box.

4. Click OK.

The marquee will now be positioned just under your sub heading. To see the final page, save the home page on your computer and view it with Internet Explorer as detailed earlier.

Adding pictures to your web page

A site with only text may be efficient and very fast loading for the viewer, but sometimes a little colour or a picture or two can make a web page far more interesting. There are two main ways in which you can use images on a web page: mixed in with text as in a magazine or as wallpaper – forming a texture or pattern in the background of the page.

Images on web pages must be in one or other of these two universal file formats:

Graphics Interchange Format (GIF or gif))

Joint Photographic Expert Group format (JPEG or jpg)

When you insert an image that is not a GIF or a JPEG – such as a BMP (bitmap) file – it is automatically converted to a GIF or a JPEG file.

For practice, try adding an image to the page normally first:

1. Place the cursor where you want the image to be placed.

2. Open the Insert menu and select Image (figure 61). Or, click the Insert Image button on the standard toolbar.

3. Either select the Clipart tab, or click on the Browse button.

4. Find an image that you have saved on your computer. You may have to open the Files of Type drop-down list to change the type of file searched for.

5. If you can't find or have not got any images of your own, browse in the Windows directory and look for files with the extension .bmp. Choose one.

6. Click Open.

Fig. 61. The Insert command. Click Image and browse for the GIF or JPEG file on your computer that you want to insert.

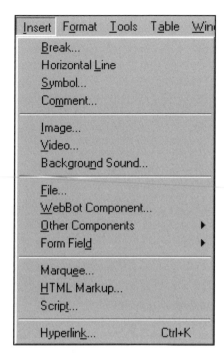

Editing the inserted image
Once you have an image on the page, you can move it around and even change its size. You can, for instance, centre the picture on the page. You can also make it act as a hyperlink so that if someone clicks the image, they will be taken to another URL (see page 78).

A common effect web designers use is to tile the background of a page with an image, giving it the appearance of having wallpaper. To do this:

1. Open the Format menu and select Background.

2. Click Specify Background and Colours.

3. Click Background Image, then Browse.

4. Select a suitable background image. Click OK.

5. Then click OK again to close the Page Properties dialog box.

Some background images can make the text on a page unreadable. Consequently, it is usually best to stick with calm images on the background. Check the image with various styles, sizes and colours of text before you finally publish it on the web.

Arranging images on a page can become extremely frustrating and confusing. If you tried to centre-align the previous image, you may have had difficulties as the image jumped round and became mixed in with the text. There is a simple answer to this problem: tables.

Using tables on a web page

An essential element in many web pages is the table. Tables are simply rows and columns of cells that can contain text, images and other components. Tables can even include other tables. Tables are a great way to arrange data or organise the whole layout of a page.

Creating a table
FrontPage Express allows you to create and format tables in many ways.

1. Create a new web page: open the File menu and select New. Select Normal Page and click OK. A blank page will appear.

2. Type a title such as 'Pictures of my family' and set the text style as Heading 1. Press enter. Now insert a 2×2 table (two columns, two rows) as follows:

3. Open the Table menu. Or, click on the Insert Table button on the standard toolbar.

4. Set the number of rows and tables to two each, and click OK. If you clicked the Insert Table button, you will see a small grid. Click on the square that is two down and two across (figure 62).

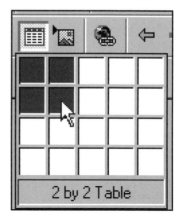

Fig. 62. The Table command allows you to select
the number of rows and columns you want.

Adding content to a table
You will now have a small table in the top left corner of the screen with the cursor flashing in the upper left cell. Type 'This is my table!' Notice that the whole table automatically resizes itself as you type. Now press the 'Tab' key or click your mouse in the upper right cell. Insert a picture of yourself, or any other image for this exercise, into the cell. The table again resizes itself.

Pressing the Tab key again moves the cursor into the lower left cell, or you can use your mouse cursor. Type 'This is my dog!' (or cat, budgie, whatever). Tab once more so that the cursor is in the lower right cell. Now

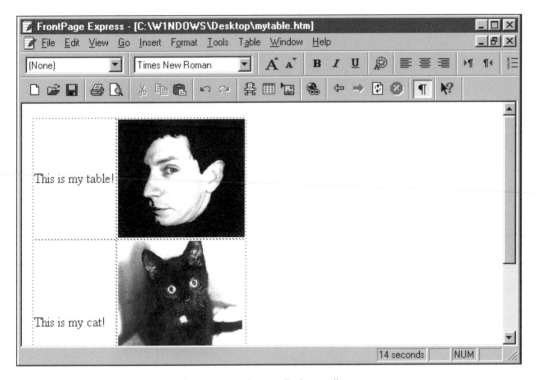

insert another picture. You now have created a small photo album on a new web page (figure 63). You could easily link to this page from your home page. Save this page as mytables.htm and keep it open (or reopen it later) to use when you read about adding links on page 78.

Fig. 63. Adding images to the cells in a table. A table helps you to lay out the appearance of your web page how you want. The table can be aligned left or right, or centred.

Refining your tables

After adding a table, you can insert table cells, rows, columns, and captions using the Table menu. You can split and merge cells, change a cell's background colour, set the size of the tables border, specify the spacing between cells, and set other table properties.

Some extra things you can do with tables (Open Table, then Table Properties):

1. Make the border visible and change the thickness and colours.

2. Use a background colour or an image inside the table.

3. Force the table to take a certain width and alignment.

Tables can be extremely complicated and are often used to control the layout of web pages so they appear well balanced – even when resized by the viewer. Take a look at Altavista.com (http://www.altavista.com/) to see some examples of how tables are used by the professionals.

▶ *Tip* – Open Altavista.com in FrontPage Express, to see better the tables and other formatting. Open the File menu and select From Location. Type in the URL http://www.altavista.com/ then, making sure you are connected to the internet, click OK.

Using FrontPage Express...

Adding some links to a web page

To add your own favourite links:

1. Add or edit an item in your hotlist.

2. Type the name of your favourite site followed by a description.

3. Select the name and open the Edit menu then select Hyperlink. You could also click on the Create Hyperlink or Edit Hyperlink button on the standard tool bar.

4. Select the World Wide Web tab and then type the URL of the site into the URL box.

5. Click OK.

Creating a link to a page in your own site
Some people have a web site of only one page. This is alright if you do not have much you want to say but for sites to be interesting to a viewer, it must have variety and be easy to read. If the amount of content on your one page is so large that a viewer has to scroll down a lengthy page for example, you should consider making several smaller pages instead. The content may neatly fall into convenient sub-sections anyway, so why not put those sub-sections on separate pages? It is usual practice to have one home page that introduces the site and which contains links to the other pages. Linking to other pages on your own site is even easier than entering links into your hot list.

Try this exercise. You should have open the page you saved earlier called 'mypage.htm' and the other called 'mytable.htm' if you have not, open them now.

1. Add an item to your page's contents list after the copyright entry.

2. Type 'My new table page'.

3. Select the text and open the Edit menu then select Hyperlink.

4. Select the World Wide Web tab and notice the list of open pages.

5. Select the MyTable entry.

6. Click OK.

7. Save MyTable and then view it with Internet Explorer and try the link.

Creating a link to a different section of the same page.
It is possible to have a hyperlink to somewhere on the same page – as in the Contents section added by the wizard. To do this, you must first create a bookmark, then a hyperlink to that bookmark. To place a bookmark, select the text you want to bookmark, open the Edit menu. You will see

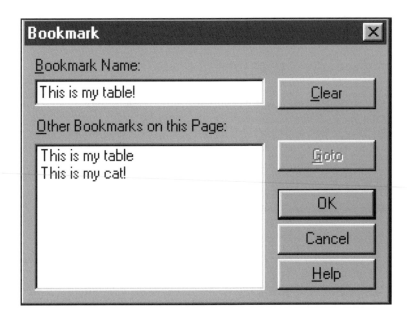

Fig. 64. Creating a link to a bookmark.

the text in the Bookmark Name box. Click OK to add it to the list of bookmarks (figure 64).

To then create a link to that bookmark, type text for the link, open the Edit menu and select Hyperlink. In the Bookmark drop-down list, select the bookmark you have created and click OK.

Practice example
Try an example:

1. Go to the copyright notice at the bottom of the page and select the word Copyright.

2. Select the text, open the Edit menu then select Bookmark.

3. Click OK to accept the name of the bookmark as Copyright. You have just created a bookmark.

4. Now go to the Contents section and add a line to the bulleted list and type Copyright notice.

5. Select the text, open the Edit menu then select Hyperlink.

6. Now on the Open pages tab click on the Bookmark drop-down list and select the Copyright entry from the list. You now have a link to the copyright notice. All you need to do is to change the text to bold to match it in with the other items in the contents.

Adding hyperlinks to images
To make an image a hyperlink is only slightly different: right-click the

image and select Image Properties. In the Default Hyperlink section of the General tab, you can type in the URL.

Some more Internet Handbooks to help you

Building a Web Site on the Internet, Brendan Murphy.
Creating a Home Page on the Internet, Richard Cochrane.

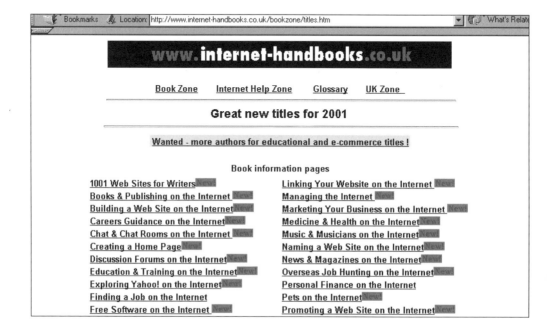

5 Security and Internet Explorer

In this chapter we will explore:

▶ *your cache*
▶ *web logs*
▶ *cookies*
▶ *hidden programs*
▶ *securing your computer*
▶ *protecting children*

. . . .

Internet Explorer was designed to enable you to enjoy exploring the internet. But it is unfortunately developing into a tool which online businesses use to spy on you. As you browse the web, Internet Explorer leaks information at the seams: big business collects that information and uses it to earn them money, either directly or by selling the information to someone else.

The information can also be a risk if someone else uses your computer. They can find out about your online habits and even 'borrow' your identity to perform illegal activities online. Security and privacy is covered more deeply in another book in the Internet Handbook series (see end of this chapter) but here are some essential basics.

Your cache

As mentioned earlier, the address and content of web pages that you have most recently visited, including the text, graphics and sound files on those pages, are stored in a special folder on your hard drive called the cache.

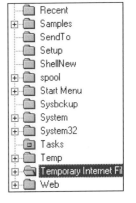

The negative result is that the cache will also provide a record of your surfing activities to the next person who uses your computer – your boss, colleagues, friends, computer engineer, your children, and your spouse. The same applies to the History list and your list of Favorites.

Web logs

Another way in which browsers leak information to others is through logs. When you view a web site, the chance is that your browser reveals certain information about you, such as who you are and what parts of the site you visit. The site then collects this information in a log. These logs are often made available to anybody who knows how to view them.

Logs may be compiled by many types of network to which your computer is connected, for example:

▶ a workplace network

▶ your school, college or university

▶ your internet service provider.

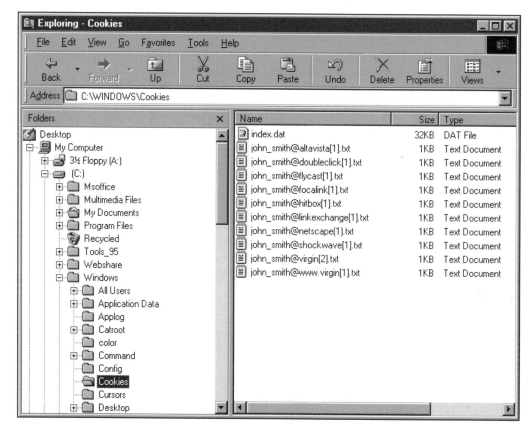

Fig. 65. A list of cookies in the Cookies folder on a Windows PC. The cookies appeared there as a result of the computer user visiting those pages.

Cookies

Internet Explorer allows web sites to store small files on your computer called cookies. These are text files that are normally stored on your computer in the following folder :

c:\windows\cookies

Cookies hold information such as your stated preferences, search keywords, your user ID, password, a list of ads you have seen, products you have bought, your name, and lots of other stuff (figure 65).

The advantages of cookies

Cookies can make browsing easier and friendlier – that's why they were originally invented. When you want to customise what you see on a particular site, a cookie can hold the information. You could ensure, for example, that you see the sports news every time you visit your favourite site. A cookie can save you from logging on to a site with your user name and password each time you visit. The possibilities are almost endless – whenever personal data needs to be saved it can be saved as a cookie.

The menace of cookies

Unfortunately, large marketing companies have turned the use of cookies around so that you the viewer are not the benefactor – they are. Thousands of sites use cookies to bug you without your knowledge or permission. They can follow every move you make on the web. The bugs obediently collect information and send it back to their 'controller' – usually a large online marketing company. This information is then sold on to other companies. In fact many of the sites are part of a larger network of sites that pool their information.

A balance of interests

Whether you see cookies as useful or an invasion of privacy depends on your viewpoint and how much you value your privacy. It is a balance between convenience and privacy; if you can do without the ability to customise how you see websites and you don't mind a little more typing then disable cookies in Internet Explorer (see page 87).

Another thought to be aware of is that the majority of search engines set cookies and some actually save your last search keywords in a cookie: be careful what you search for, you might get more than you wanted.

▶ *Tip* – Microsoft, at time of writing, is testing a cookie management feature. The new manager will tell users when web sites offer them cookies, and make it easier for users to delete and manage them.

Hidden programs

Modern browsers are far more than just document viewers. They can also allow web pages to perform complicated tasks on the web, or even on your own computer.

▶ *Program* – A computer program is a series of coded instructions designed to automatically control a computer in carrying out a specific task. Programs are written in special languages including Java, JavaScript, VBScript, and ActiveX.

Embedded in some web pages are certain programs. When you view one of these pages, your browser downloads the programs along with the rest of the contents. Once one of these programs is on your computer, your browser interprets the instructions and carries them out.

Many of these programs are not harmful. On the contrary, they can be extremely useful. But in the hands of someone who has a little knowledge, a lot of damage can be caused such as deleting files or collecting private information.

There are three main types of program:

1. scripts

2. applets

3. controls

Security and Internet Explorer..

Scripts

A script is a set of commands written into the HTML tags of a web page (see figure 66). Script languages such as JavaScript and VBScript work rather like macros in a word processor. Scripts are hidden from view but are executed when you open a page or click a link containing script instructions. Scripts are common and mostly harmless, but JavaScript was never tested properly and contains many weaknesses that can be exploited.

Some of the first were discovered by a 15-year-old who found them by accident. Since then, many more bugs have been discovered. In the wrong hands, JavaScript can perform malicious tasks like capturing your username and password – and worse. For more information see:

Fig. 66. A script is a set of commands written into the HTML tags of a web page.

http://www.geek-girl.com/bugtraq/1998_1/0218.html

```
<script language="JavaScript">
<!--
    popup('http://doc.altavista.com/popups/uk.html',400,300);
    function popup(page, width, height) {
        var tmp;
        if (oPopupWin) {
            tmp = oPopupWin;
            oPopupWin = null;
            if (navigator.appName != "Netscape")
                tmp.close();
        }
        oPopupWin = window.open(page, "IntlPopup",
"alwaysRaised=1,dependent=1,height=" + height +
",location=0,menubar=0,personalbar=0,scrollbars=0,status=0,toolbar=0,w
idth=" + width + ",resizable=0");
        oPopupWin.focus();
        return !oPopupWin;
    }
    var oPopupWin;
// -->
</script>
```

Java applets

Whereas JavaScript is contained in a web page, programs written in Java are in separate files called applets. Java is a much more complicated, and powerful, language. It can perform correspondingly more complicated and spectacular tasks.

▶ *Example* – It could be a financial calculator that keeps track of the rate of exchange of various currencies in real time. The application could refer to the web site for up-to-the-minute rates and let you calculate accordingly.

Most Java applets are useful, or at least harmless. Sometimes, however, they can cause serious damage. There have been cases of Java causing computers to reboot and thus lose all unsaved data. But not even Java is the biggest threat to security: ActiveX is the real villain.

ActiveX

Microsoft's answer to Java and JavaScript was ActiveX. Sites with ActiveX components can often display the most stunning effects and useful features. However, it can be used maliciously to devastating effect.

▶ *Example* – An ActiveX component could easily be written to scan your computer for all documents. It could then send those documents to someone else without your knowledge. A malicious programmer could easily install a computer virus on a system, turn off all the security features, and read your personal files. He could then upload them secretly to a remote web site, delete document files from your hard drive, and remove system files so that your system will no longer start. (Source: *Risks Digest 20.50* posted on the Usenet risks newsgroup – comp.risks).

Securing your computer

Internet Explorer
We all think that we have little to worry about, that no one can get into our computer and access the personal information we have there. It may be that your computer is physically secure – but is that enough?

▶ *Example* – Suppose you have recently visited an online bookshop and bought a book. You logged in and then entered your credit card details. The site will be recorded in your History list. If someone else opens your History list and visits that site, it is very likely that either AutoComplete or a cookie will remember your login name, password and even credit card details. What's more, if they use Outlook Express, they will be able to send messages in your name – to engage in anything from practical jokes to forgery and hacking.

Even members of your family or trusted work colleagues might be tempted to use your personal information when filling in forms on the internet. There is a case where an American youth bought a $100,000 sports car using his father's account.

Stretch the scenario a step further and you may see that even if you keep your computer in a locked room it is still possible for your personal details to be used to make a purchase from one of your regular online stores – using ActiveX to unlock your computer.

In January 1997 members of a group called the Chaos Computer Club showed how an ActiveX program could take control of a PC and transfer funds from an online bank account without the user's knowledge. Disable ActiveX on your computer, if you do nothing else.

If you still believe that you have nothing to worry about, go to Richard M Smith's web page (figure 67):

http://www.tiac.net/users/smiths/acctroj/axcheck.htm

Security and Internet Explorer...

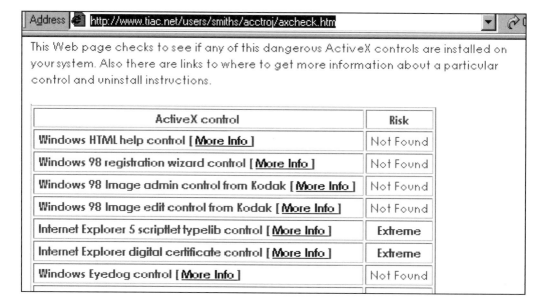

ActiveX control	Risk
Windows HTML help control [**More Info**]	Not Found
Windows 98 registration wizard control [**More Info**]	Not Found
Windows 98 Image admin control from Kodak [**More Info**]	Not Found
Windows 98 Image edit control from Kodak [**More Info**]	Not Found
Internet Explorer 5 scriptlet typelib control [**More Info**]	Extreme
Internet Explorer digital certificate control [**More Info**]	Extreme
Windows Eyedog control [**More Info**]	Not Found

Fig. 67. Richard M Smith's web page will tell you more about the risks of ActiveX.

Now test your system for vulnerabilities and run a few demonstrations – the demos are safe but they graphically illustrate what could happen.

Outlook Express

Outlook Express is not immune, either. A security expert managed to construct a test email message containing a few lines of JavaScript that runs when a message is viewed. The script indirectly downloads a Windows executable file, installs it on the hard drive then executes it. For his test he downloaded and ran the Windows calculator program but the same method could be used to run a virus or any other harmful program. Many of the new types of virus depend on this vulnerability.

Outlook Express security is dependent on Internet Explorer and, if you have them, Microsoft Office programs. It can only be made secure by a complicated set of precautions involving Outlook Express, Internet Explorer and Office.

Making Outlook Express more secure
You can adjust security settings within Outlook Express:

1. Select the Tools menu, then Options (figure 68).

2. Click the Security tab.

3. There, you will find that you can set Outlook to use one of two security zones: Internet and Restricted Sites Zone.

By default, messages are viewed in the internet zone in which messages containing JavaScript code, ActiveX controls, or Java applets are automatically executed when a message is read. So almost all the problems associated with scripts and ActiveX components can be initiated in an HTML email message.

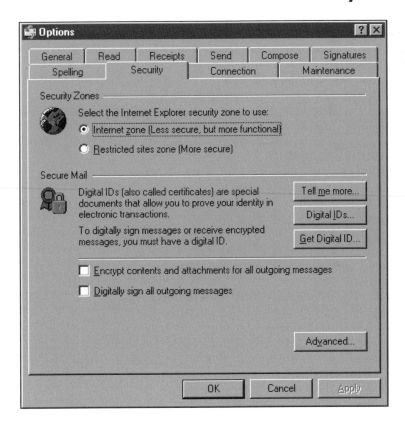

Fig. 68. Adjusting the
security settings in
Outlook Express.

The second security zone – Restricted sites – turns off ActiveX and Java support and supposedly offers greater security. However, it still allows JavaScript to run and Microsoft Office documents may still open without any warnings.

A malicious person can send you a message with a line or two of script that opens a browser window, and, incredibly, that window is then run in the internet security zone and can thus run harmful Java and ActiveX controls. Alternatively, they can send you a Word document infected with a macro virus and, if you have not configured Word properly, your computer will be infected.

To make Outlook Express safe, you *must* change the settings within Internet Explorer.

Making Internet Explorer safe

To disable the various features:

1. Open the Tools menu.

2. Select Internet Options then the Security tab.

3. Select the Internet zone.

4. Click the Custom level button.

Fig. 69. Disabling 'Script ActiveX controls marked safe for scripting'. This will disable ActiveX and Java in Internet Explorer.

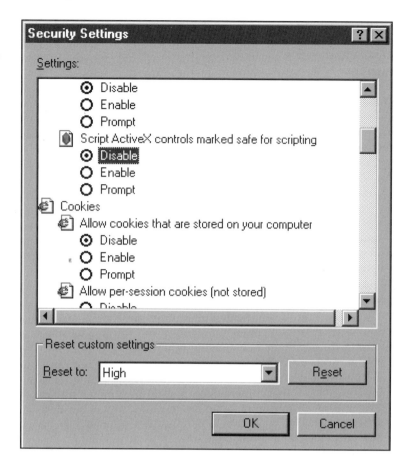

5. Disable 'Script ActiveX controls marked safe for scripting'. This will disable ActiveX and Java (figure 69).

Unfortunately, some web sites blackmail you into giving them information by refusing to 'let you in' if the features mentioned above – cookies, Javascript, ActiveX – are disabled. It is your choice whether or not to yield to them. If you do, be very careful about what information you give away. Back up your important data to protect yourself in the event of coming across a more malicious site.

Protecting children

A computer in a child's bedroom is no longer merely a computer. As soon as it is connected to the internet, it becomes a doorway that practically anyone in the world can use to enter your child's bedroom – without your knowledge.

As soon as children are able to use a computer keyboard and connect to the web, they are at risk from unscrupulous websites or individuals. However, teenagers are more at risk than younger children because they often use the computer unsupervised.

There are, for example, areas on the internet where children would encounter people of an extreme nature and may suffer prejudice, hatred, threats or harassment. Another risk is that your children may come in contact with pornographic material or content that encourages dangerous or illegal activities. Your child, out of mischief or ignorance, might even use your personal information on the net. The combination of a child, a credit card and an online auction, for example, is enough to make any parent shiver.

How do you guard against these risks? These are some of the commonly used methods:

1. filtering software

2. ratings system

3. parental control

Filtering software is used to block or screen unsuitable material and also prevents your address, phone and credit card numbers from being given out on the internet. Some software is capable of monitoring the web, email, chat programs, newsgroups and offline applications and gives you control over what is being accessed.

You determine the levels and areas of access for each user. You can allow full access, or deny access altogether.

The ratings system is similar, but Internet Explorer acts as the filtering system and websites give themselves a rating depending on the type of sexual and violent content. In Internet Explorer, you can find the rating system in Tools, Internet Options, Content and Content Advisor. Once you enable Content Advisor, a password is needed to bypass it.

The main problem with ratings and filtering software is that it often cuts out so many web sites that the browsing experience is useless to the intelligent teenager. What is worse, some of the filtering companies ban sites that criticise their software and at the same time try to hide the fact. Besides, teenagers will probably know more than you do about the internet and will be able to bypass any restrictions you put on the computer. See the Peacefire site at for the truth behind filtering software – how they are not in the interests of children and are easily bypassed anyway (figure 70):

http://www.peacefire.org

The only practical alternative relies on parental guidance and education. As with a television, if a computer is in the child's bedroom, there is no foolproof way of ensuring that your child is not accessing something dubious or harmful.

▶ Sharing the experience of the internet with your children will help you obtain the full benefits of the internet and alert you to any potential problems that may await your child.

▶ Never allow the computer to stay in a child's bedroom. Besides making the child less sociable, it can be an open invitation for any

Security and Internet Explorer...

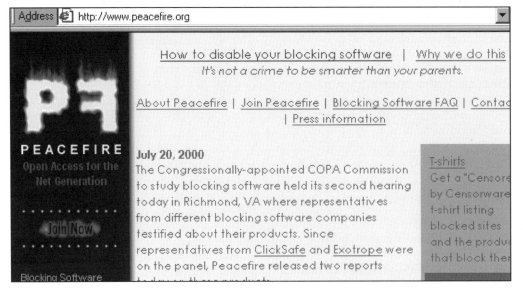

Address 📄 http://www.peacefire.org ▼

How to disable your blocking software | Why we do this
It's not a crime to be smarter than your parents.

About Peacefire | Join Peacefire | Blocking Software FAQ | Contac
| Press information

PEACEFIRE
Open Access for the
Net Generation

. . . .
Join Now
. . . .

Blocking Software

July 20, 2000
The Congressionally-appointed COPA Commission
to study blocking software held its second hearing
today in Richmond, VA where representatives
from different blocking software companies
testified about their products. Since
representatives from ClickSafe and Exotrope were
on the panel, Peacefire released two reports

T-shirts
Get a "Censore
by Censorware
t-shirt listing
blocked sites
and the produ
that block the

Fig. 70. See the Peacefire site for the truth behind filtering software. As you will discover, there are no simple answers to filtering out unwelcome material.

stranger. Keep the computer in a shared room and keep an eye on what is happening or, even better, join in. If all else fails, you can lock it away when you leave the child alone in the house for any length or time.

▶ Educate your children so that they know not to give out personal information such as name, address, phone number, email address and school address to anyone or any site on the internet without talking to you first.

▶ You may have taught your child to avoid strangers in the street, but what is a stranger on the internet? You need to make sure that your child understands that a web site can collect information by using cartoon characters to act as representatives. Would your child trust his favourite cartoon character? How can the child see a red fluffy bunny or a funny-faced clown as being harmful in any way?

In the new global age of the internet, it is incumbent on all users to equip themselves with the right skills to use it in a responsible and safe fashion.

More Internet Handbooks to help you

Protecting Children on the Internet: An effective approach for parents and teachers, Graham Jones (Internet Handbooks).

Your Privacy on the Internet: Everything you need to know about protecting your privacy and security online, Kye Valongo (Internet Handbooks).

Some essential web sites

History of the internet

The History of the Internet
http://www.pbs.org/internet/timeline/

A Short History of the Internet
info.isoc.org/guest/zakon/Internet/History/Short_History_of_the_Internet

Getting connected

Directory of Free ISPs
http://www.a2zweblinks.com/freeukisp/index.htm

Macintosh: Open Transport Help
http://www2.netdoor.com/~rreid/opentransport/

Windows: How to Set Up A Winsock Connection – A Beginner's Guide
http://omni.cc.purdue.edu/~xniu/winsock.htm

The world wide web

Newbie U's Web Stadium
http://www.newbie-u.com/web/

All About the World Wide Web
http://www.imaginarylandscape.com/helpweb/www/www.html

Sink or Swim: Internet Search Tools & Techniques
http://www.ouc.bc.ca/libr/connect96/search.htm

Search Engine Shoot-out: Search Engines Compared
http://www.cnet.com/Content/Reviews/Compare/Search2/

Email

Everything E-mail
http://everythingemail.net/

A Beginner's Guide to Effective Email
http://www.webfoot.com/advice/email.top.html

How to find people's Email addresses
http://www.qucis.queensu.ca/FAQs/email/finding.html

Some essential web sites ....

Discussion forums

Email Discussion Groups/Lists – Resources
http://www.webcom.com/impulse/list.html

The List of Lists
http://catalog.com/vivian/interest-group-search.html

Privacy and security on the internet

Electronic Privacy Information Centre (EPIC)
http://www.epic.org
EPIC is a research centre in Washington. It was established in 1994 to focus public attention on civil liberties issues and to protect privacy, the First Amendment and constitutional values. EPIC works in association with the London human rights group Privacy International.

Internet Freedom
http://www.netfreedom.org
Internet Freedom is opposed to all forms of censorship and content regulation on the net. The site mainly consists of news about the many forms of censorship.

Privacy International
http://www.privacyinternational.org
Their site says: 'Privacy International is a human rights group formed in 1990 as a watchdog on surveillance by governments and corporations. PI is based in London, and has an office in Washington, D.C. PI has conducted campaigns in Europe, Asia and North America to counter abuses of privacy by way of information technology such as telephone tapping, ID card systems, video surveillance, data matching, police information systems, and medical records.'

Privacy Rights Clearing House
http://www.privacyrights.org
The PRC is a site that provides in-depth information on a variety of informational privacy issues, as well as giving tips on safeguarding your personal privacy. The PRC was established with funding from the Telecommunications Education Trust, a program of the California Public Utilities Commission.

Glossary of internet terms

access provider The company that provides you with access to the internet. This may be an independent provider or a large international organisation such as AOL or CompuServe. See also **internet service provider**.

ActiveX A Microsoft programming language that allows effects such as animations, games and other interactive features to be included a web page.

Adobe Acrobat A type of software required for reading PDF files ('portable document format'). You may need to have Adobe Acrobat Reader when downloading large text files from the internet, such as lengthy reports or chapters from books. If your computer lacks it, the web page will prompt you, and usually offer you an immediate download of the free version.

address book A directory in a web browser where you can store people's email addresses. This saves having to type them out each time you want to email someone. You just click on an address whenever you want it.

ADSL Stands for Asymmetric Digital Subscriber Line. It is a new phone line technology developed by British Telecommunications in the UK to provide an internet connection speed up to ten times faster than a typical modem.

Adult check An age verification system that only allows the over 18s to enter adult web sites.

affiliate programme A system that allows you to sell other companies products via your web site.

age verification Commercial systems that prevent minors from accessing adult oriented web sites.

AltaVista One of the half dozen most popular internet search engines. Just type in a few key words to find what you want on the internet. See: http://www.altavista.com

AOL America On Line, the world's biggest internet service provider, with more than 25 million subscribers, and now merged with Time Warner. Because it has masses of content of its own – quite aside from the wider internet – it is sometimes referred to as an 'online' service provider rather than internet service provider. It has given away vast numbers of free CDs with the popular computer magazines to build its customer base. See: http://www.aol.com

Apple Macintosh A type of computer that has its own proprietary operating system, as distinct from the MSDOS and Windows operating systems found on PCs (personal computers). The Apple Mac has long been a favourite of designers and publishers.

applet An application programmed in Java that is designed to run only on a web browser. Applets cannot read or write data onto your computer, only from the domain in which they are served from. When a web page using an applet is accessed, the browser will download it and run it on your computer. See also **Java** .

application Any program, such as a word processor or spreadsheet program, designed for use on your computer.

application service provider A company that provides computer software via the internet, whereby the application is borrowed, rather than downloaded. You keep your data, they keep the program.

ARPANET Advanced Research Projects Agency Network, an early form of the internet.

ASCII American Standard Code for Information Interchange. It is a simple text file format that can be accessed by most word processors and text editors. It is a universal file type for passing textual information across the internet.

Ask Jeeves A popular internet search engine. Rather than just typing in a few key words for your search, you can type in a whole question or instruction, such as 'Find me everything about online investment.' It draws on a database of millions of questions and answers, and works best with fairly general questions.

ASP (1) Active server page, a filename extension for a type of web page. (2) Application service provider (see above),

attachment A file sent with an email message. The attached file can be anything from a word-processed document to a database, spreadsheet, graphic, or even a sound or video file. For example you could email someone birthday greetings, and attach a sound track or video clip.

Authenticode Authenticode is a system where ActiveX controls can be authenticated in some way, usually by a certificate.

avatar A cartoon or image used to represent someone on screen while taking part in internet chat.

backup A second copy of a file or a set of files. Backing up data is essential if there is any risk of data loss.

bandwidth The width of the electronic highway that gives you access to the internet. The higher the bandwidth, the wider this highway, and the faster the traffic can flow.

banner ad This is a band of text and graphics, usually situated at the top of a web page. It acts like a title, telling the user what the content of the page is about. It invites the visitor to click on it to visit that site. Banner advertising has become big business.

baud rate The data transmission speed in a modem, measured in bps (bits per second).

BBS Bulletin board service. A facility to read and to post public messages on a particular web site.

binary numbers The numbering system used by computers. It only uses 1s and 0s to represent numbers. Decimal numbers are based on the number 10. You can count from nought to nine. When you count higher than nine, the nine is replaced with a 10. Binary numbers are based on the number 2: each place can only have the value of 1 or 0.

Blue Ribbon Campaign A widely supported campaign supporting free speech and opposing moves to censor the internet by all kinds of elected and unelected bodies. See the Electronic Frontier Foundation at: http://www.eff.org

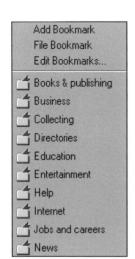

bookmark A file of URLs of your favourite internet sites. Bookmarks are very easily created by saving the address of any internet page you like the look of. If you are an avid user, you could soon end up with hundreds of them! In the Internet Explorer browser and AOL they are called Favorites.

boolean search A search in which you type in words such as AND and OR to refine your search. Such words are called 'Boolean operators'. The concept is named after George Boole, a nineteenth-century English mathematician.

bot Short for robot. It is used to refer to a program that will perform a task on the internet, such as carrying out a search.

brokers Online agencies that buy and sell domain names.

browser Your browser is your window to the internet, and will normally supplied by your internet service provider when you first sign up. It is the program that you use to access the world wide web, and manage your personal communications and privacy when online. By far the two most popular browsers are Netscape Communicator and its dominant rival Microsoft Internet Explorer. You can easily swap. Both can be downloaded free from their web sites and are found on the CD roms stuck to the computer magazines. It won't make much difference which one you use – they both do much the same thing. Opera, at http://www.opera.com is a great alternative that improves security, is faster and more efficient.

bug A weakness in a program or a computer system.

bulletin board A type of computer-based news service that provides an email service and a file archive.

cache A file storage area on a computer. Your web browser will normally cache (copy to your hard drive) each web page you visit. When you revisit that page on the web, you may in fact be looking at the page originally cached on your computer. To be sure you are viewing the current page, press **reload** or **refresh** on your browser toolbar. You can empty your cache from time to time, and the computer will do so automatically whenever the cache is full. In Internet Explorer, pages are saved in the Windows folder, Temporary Internet Files. In Netscape they are saved in a folder called 'cache'.

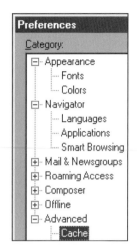

certificate A computer file that securely identifies a person or organisation on the internet.

CGI Common gateway interface. This defines how the web server should pass information to the program, such as what it's being asked to do, what objects it should work with, any inputs, and so on. It is the same for all web servers.

channel (chat) Place where you can chat with other internet chatters. The name of a chat channel is prefixed with a hash mark, #.

click stream The sequence of hyperlinks clicked by someone when using the internet.

click through This is when someone clicks on a banner ad or other link, for example, and is moved from that page to the advertiser's web site.

client This is the term given to the program that you use to access the internet. For example your web browser is a web client, and your email program is an email client.

colocating Putting your computer at another company's location so you can connect your web site permanently to the internet.

community The internet is often described as a net community. This refers to the fact that many people like the feeling of belonging to a group of like-minded individuals. Many big web sites have been developed along these lines, such as GeoCities which is divided into special-interest 'neighbourhoods', or America OnLine which is strong on member services.

compression Computer files can be electronically compressed, so that they can be uploaded or downloaded more quickly across the internet, saving time and money. If an image file is compressed too much, there may be a loss of quality. To read compressed files, you uncompress – 'unzip' – them.

configure To set up, or adjust the settings, of a computer or software program.

content Articles, columns, sales messages, images, and the text of your web site.

content services Web sites dedicated to a particular subject.

cookie A cookie is a small file that the server asks your browser to keep until it asks for it. If it sends it with the first page and asks for it back before each other page, they can follow you around the site, even if you switch your computer off in between.

cracker Someone who breaks into computer systems with the intention of causing some kind of damage or abusing the system in some way.

crash What happens when a computer program malfunctions. The operating system of your PC may perform incorrectly or come to a complete stop ('freeze'), forcing you to shut down and restart.

cross-posting Posting an identical message in several different newsgroups at the same time.

cybercash This is a trademark, but is also often used as a broad term to describe the use of small payments made over the internet using a new form of electronic account that is loaded up with cash. You can send this money to the companies offering such cash facilities by cheque, or by credit card. Some internet companies offering travel-related items can accept electronic cash of this kind.

cyberspace Popular term for the intangible 'place' where you go to surf – the ethereal and borderless world of computers and telecommunications on the internet.

cypherpunk From the cypherpunk mailing list charter: 'Cypherpunks assume privacy is a good thing and wish there were more of it. Cypherpunks acknowledge that those who want privacy must create it for themselves and not expect governments, corporations, or other large, faceless organisations to grant them privacy out of beneficence. Cypherpunks know that people have been creating their own privacy for centuries with whispers, envelopes, closed doors, and couriers. Cypherpunks do not seek to prevent other people from speaking about their experiences or their opinions.'

cypherpunk remailer Cypherpunk remailers strip headers from the messages and add new ones.

cybersquatting Using someone else's name or trademark as your domain name in the hope they will buy it from you

cyberstalker An individual who pursues a victim using email, chat rooms and newsgroups. Often attempting to arrange a meeting with children.

data Information. Data can exist in many forms such as numbers in a spreadsheet, text in a document, or as binary numbers stored in a computer's memory.

database A store of information in digital form. Many web sites make use of substantial databases to deliver maximum content at high speed to the web user.

dial up account This allows you to connect your computer to your internet provider's computer remotely.

digital Based on the two binary digits, 1 and 0. The operation of all computers is based on this amazingly simple concept. All forms of information are capable of being digitised – numbers, words, and even sounds and images – and then transmitted over the internet.

digital signature A unique personal signature specially created for use over the internet, designed to take the place of the traditional handwritten signature.

directory On a PC, a folder containing your files.

DNS Domain name server.

domain name A name that identifies an IP address. It identifies to the computers on the rest of the internet where to access particular information. Each domain has a name. For someone@somewhere.co.uk, 'somewhere' is the domain name.

download Downloading means copying a file from one computer on the internet to your own computer. You do this by clicking on a button that links you to the appropriate file. Downloading is an automatic process, except that you have to click 'yes' to accept the download and give it a file name. You can download any type of file – text, graphics, sound, spreadsheet, computer programs, and so on.

ebusiness The broad concept of doing business to business, and business to consumer sales, over the internet.

ecash Short for electronic cash. See cybercash.

ecommerce The various means and techniques of transacting business online.

Echelon The name of a massive governmental surveillance facility based in Yorkshire, UK. Operated clandestinely by the US, UK and certain other governments, it is said to be eavesdropping virtually the entire traffic of the internet. It is said to use special electronic dictionaries to trawl through millions of emails and other transmissions.

ecommerce The various means and techniques of transacting business online.

Dial-Up
Networking

email Electronic mail, any message or file you send from your computer to another computer using your 'email client' program (such as Netscape Messenger or Microsoft Outlook).

email address The unique address given to you by your ISP. It can be used by others using the internet to send email messages to you. An example of a standard email address is:

mybusiness@aol.com

email bomb An attack by email where you are sent hundreds or thousands of email messages in a very short period. This attack often prevents you receiving genuine email messages.

emoticons Popular symbols used to express emotions in email, for example the well-known smiley :-) which means 'I'm smiling!' Emoticons are not normally appropriate for business communications.

encryption The scrambling of information to make it unreadable without a key or password. Email and any other data can now be encrypted using PGP and other freely available programs. Modern encryption has become so amazingly powerful as to be to all intents and purposes uncrackable. Law enforcers world wide are pressing their governments for access to people's and organisation's passwords and security keys. Would you be willing to hand over yours?

Excite A popular internet directory and search engine used to find pages relating to specific keywords which you enter. See: http://www.excite.com

ezines The term for magazines and newsletters published on the internet.

FAQs Frequently asked questions. You will see 'FAQ' everywhere you go on the internet. If you are ever doubtful about anything check the FAQ page, if the site has one, and you should find the answers to your queries.

Favorites The rather coy term for **bookmarks** used by Internet Explorer, and by America Online. Maintaining a list of Favourites is designed to make returning to a site easier.

file A file is any body of data such as a word processed document, a spreadsheet, a database file, a graphics or video file, sound file, or computer program. On a PC, a file has a filename, and filename extension showing what type of file it is.

filtering software Software loaded onto a computer to prevent access by someone to unwelcome content on the internet, notably porn. The well-known 'parental controls' include CyberSitter, CyberPatrol, SurfWatch and NetNanny. They can be blunt instruments. For example, if they are programmed to reject all web pages containing the word 'virgin', you would not be able to access any web page hosted at Richard Branson's Virgin Net! Of course, there are also web sites that tell you step-by-step how to disable or bypass these filtering tools, such as: http://www.peacefire.org

finger A tool for locating people on the internet. The most common use is to see if a person has an account at a particular internet site. Also, a chat command that returns information about the other chat user, including idle time (time since they last did anything).

firewall A firewall is special security software designed to stop the flow of certain files into and out of a computer network, e.g. viruses or attacks by hackers. A firewall would be an important feature of any fully commercial web site.

flame A more or less hostile or aggressive message posted in a newsgroup or to an individual newsgroup user. If they get out of hand there can be flame wars.

folder The name for a directory on a computer. It is a place in which files are stored.

form A web page that allows or requires you to enter information into fields on the page and send the information to a web site, program or individual on the web. Forms are often used for registration or sending questions and com-

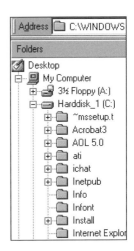

ments to web sites.

forums Places for discussion on the internet. They include Usenet newsgroups, mailing lists, and bulletin board services.

frames A web design feature in which web pages are divided into several areas or panels, each containing separate information. A typical set of frames in a page includes an index frame (with navigation links), a banner frame (for a heading), and a body frame (for text matter).

freebies The 'give away' products, services or other enticements offered on a web site to attract registrations.

freespace An allocation of free web space by an internet service provider or other organisation, to its users or subscribers.

freeware Software programs made available without charge. Where a small charge is requested, the term is **shareware**.

front page The first page of your web site that the visitor will see. FrontPage is also the name of a popular web authoring package from Microsoft.

FTP File transfer protocol – the method the internet uses to speed files back and forth between computers. Your browser will automatically select this method, for instance, when you want to download your bank statements to reconcile your accounts. In practice you don't need to worry about FTP unless you are thinking about creating and publishing your own web pages: then you would need some of the freely available FTP software. Despite the name, it's easy to use.

GIF Graphic interchange format. It is a widely-used compressed file format used on web pages and elsewhere to display files that contain graphic images. See also **JPEG** and **PDF**.

graphical client A graphical client typically uses many windows, one for each conversation you are involved in. Each window has a command line and status bar.

GUI Short for graphic user interface. It describes the user-friendly screens found in Windows and other WIMP environments (Windows, icons, mice, pointers).

hacker A person interested in computer programming, operating systems, the internet and computer security. The term can be used to describe a person who breaks into computer systems with the intention of pointing out the weaknesses in a system. In common usage, the term is often wrongly used to describe crackers.

header The header is that part of a message which contains information about the sender and the route that the message took through the internet.

History list A record of visited web pages. Your browser probably includes a history list. It is handy way of revisiting sites whose addresses you have forgotten to bookmark – just click on the item you want in the history list. You can normally delete all or part of the history list in your browser. However, your ISP may well be keeping web logs even if you delete it on your own computer (see **internet service providers**, above).

hit counter A piece of software used by a web site to record the number of hits it has received.

hits The number of times items on a web site have been viewed.

home page This refers to the index page of an individual or an organisation on the internet. It usually contains links to related pages of information, and to other relevant sites

host A host is the computer where a particular file or domain is located, and from where people can retrieve it.

HotBot A popular internet search engine used to find pages relating to any keywords you decide to enter.

HTML Hyper text markup language, the universal computer language used to create pages on the world wide web. It is much like word processing, but uses special 'tags' for formatting the text and creating hyperlinks to other web pages.

HTTP Hypertext transfer protocol, the protocol used by the world wide web. It is the language spoken between your browser and the web servers. It is the standard way that HTML documents are transferred from host computer to your local browser when you're surfing the internet. You'll see this acronym at the start of every web address, for example:

http://www.abcxyz.com

With modern browsers, it is no longer necessary to enter 'http://' at the start of the address.

hyperlink See **link** .

hypertext This is a link on an HTML page that, when clicked with a mouse, results in a further HTML page or graphic being loaded into view on your browser.

IANA The Internet Assigned Numbers Authority, the official body responsible for ensuring that the numerical coding of the internet works properly,

ICANN The committee that oversees the whole domain name system.

ICQ A form of internet chat, derived from the phrase 'I seek you'. It enables users to be alerted whenever fellow users go online, so they can have instant chat communication. The proprietary software is now owned by America Online.

impression An internet advertising term that means the showing of a single instance of an advert on a single computer screen.

Infoseek One of the ten most popular internet search engines.

Intel Manufacturer of the Pentium, Celeron and other microprocessors.

internet The broad term for the fast-expanding network of global computers that can access each other in seconds by phone and satellite links. If you are using a modem on your computer, you too are part of the internet. The general term 'internet' encompasses email, web pages, internet chat, newsgroups, mailing lists, bulletin boards, and video conferencing. It is rather like the way we speak of 'the printed word' when we mean books, magazines, newspapers, news-letters, catalogues, leaflets, tickets and posters. The 'internet' does not exist in one place any more than 'the printed word' does.

internet2 A new form of the internet being developed exclusively for educational and academic use.

internet account The account set up by your internet service provider which gives you access to the world wide web, electronic mail facilities, newsgroups and other value added services.

internet directory A special web site which consists of information about other sites. The information is classified by subject area and further subdivided into smaller categories. The biggest and most widely used is Yahoo! at: http://www.yahoo.com See also **search engines**.

Internet Explorer The world's most popular browser software, a product of Microsoft and leading the field against Netscape (now owned by America Online).

internet keywords A commercial service that allows people to find your domain name without having to type in www or .com

Internet protocol number The numerical code that is your real domain name address.

internet service providers ISPs are commercial, educational or official organi-sations which offer people ('users') access to the internet. The well-known commercial ones in the UK include AOL, CompuServe, BT Internet, Freeserve, Demon and Virgin Net. Commercial ISPs may levy a fixed monthly charge, though the worldwide trend is now towards free services. Services typically include access to the world wide web, email and newsgroups, as well as others such as news, chat, and entertainment. Your internet service provider will probably know everything you do on the internet – emails sent and received, web sites visited, information downloaded, key words typed into search engines, newsgroups visited and messages read and posted. This is why many of them are willing to offer their services free. What do they do with all this data? How long do they store it? Do they make it discreetly available to government agencies? There are some major issues of personal privacy and data protection in all this, at both a national and European level, and state surveillance is expanding fast. At the very least, check out your service provider's privacy statement – but it may mean very little.

intranet Software that uses internet technology to allow communication between individuals, for example within a large commercial organisation. It often operates on a LAN (local area network).

IP address An 'internet protocol' address. All computers linked to the internet have one. The address is somewhat like a telephone number, and consists of four sets of numbers separated by dots.

IPv6 The new internet coding system that will allow even more domain names.

IRC Internet relay chat. Chat is an enormously popular part of the internet, and there are all kinds of chat rooms and chat software. The chat involves typing messages which are sent and read in real time. It was developed in 1988 by a Finn called Jarkko Oikarinen.

ISDN Integrated Services Digital Network. This is a high-speed telephone network that can send computer data from the internet to your PC faster than a normal telephone line.

Java A programming language developed by Sun Microsystems to use the special properties of the internet to create graphics and multimedia applications on web sites.

JavaScript A simple programming language that can be put onto a web page to create interactive effects such as buttons that change appearance when you position the mouse over them.

JPEG The acronym is short for Joint Photographic Experts Group. A JPEG is a specialised file format used to display graphic files on the internet. JPEG files are smaller than similar GIF files and so have become ever more popular – even though there is sometimes a feeling that their quality is not as good as GIF format files. See also MPEG.

key shortcut Two keys pressed at the same time. Usually the 'control' key (Ctrl), 'Alt' key, or 'Shift' key combined with a letter or number. For example to use 'Control-D', press 'Control', tap the 'D' key once firmly then take your finger off the 'Control' key.

keywords Words that sum up your web site for being indexed in search engines. For example for a cosmetic site the key words might include beauty, lipstick, make-up, fashion, cosmetic and so on.

kick To eject someone from a chat channel.

LAN A local area network, a computer network usually located in one building or campus.

link A hypertext phrase or image that calls up another web page when you click on it. Most web sites have lots of hyperlinks, or 'links' for short. These appear on the screen as buttons, images or bits of text (often underlined) that you can click on with your mouse to jump to another site on the world wide web.

Linux A new widely and freely available operating system for personal computers, and a potentially serious challenger to Microsoft. It has developed a considerable following.

LINX The London Internet Exchange, the facility which maintains UK internet traffic in the UK. It allows existing individual internet service providers to exchange traffic within the UK, and improve connectivity and service for their customers. LINX is one of the largest and fastest growing exchange

Quick Click Menu

Site Map
IRC Introduction
Newbies FAQ
IRC & Web Security

IRC Network Basics
IRC Networks
IRC Commands

mIRC Central
mIRC Installation

points in Europe, and maintains connectivity between the UK and the rest of the world.

listserver An automated email system whereby subscribers are able to receive and send email from other subscribers to the list.

log on/log off To access/leave a network. In the early days of computing this literally involved writing a record in a log book. You may be asked to 'log on' to certain sites and particular pages. This normally means entering your user ID in the form of a name and a password.

lurk The slang term used to describe reading a newsgroup's messages without actually taking part in that newsgroup. Despite the connotations of the word, it is a perfectly respectable activity on the internet.

macros 'Macro languages' are used to automate repetitive tasks in Word processors and other applications.

mail server A remote computer that enables you to send and receive emails. Your internet access provider will usually act as your mail server.

mailing list A forum where messages are distributed by email to the members of the forum. The two types of lists are discussion and announcement. Discussion lists allow exchange between list members. Announcement lists are one-way only and used to distribute information such as news or humour. A good place to find mailing lists is Liszt (http://www.liszt.com). You can normally quit a mailing list by sending an email message to request removal.

marquee A moving (scrolling) line of text on a web site.

Media Player Software on a personal computer that will play sounds and images including video clips and animations.

metasearch engine A site that sends a keyword search to many different search engines and directories so you can use many search engines from one place.

meta tags The technical term for the keywords used in your web page code to help search engine software rank your site.

Microsoft The world's biggest producer of software for personal computers, including the Windows operating systems, and the web browser Internet Explorer.

Mixmaster An anonymous remailer that sends and receives email messages as packages of exactly the same size and often randomly varies the delay time between receiving and remailing to make interception harder.

modem This is an internal or external piece of hardware plugged into your PC. It links into a standard phone socket, thereby giving you access to the internet. The word derives from MOdulator/DEModulator.

moderator A person in charge of a mailing list, newsgroup or forum. The moderator prevents unwanted messages.

mpeg or **mpg** The file format used for video clips available on the internet. See also JPEG. See http://mpeg.org for further technical information

MP3 An immensely popular audio format that allows you to download and play music on your computer. It compresses music to create files that are small yet whose quality is almost as good as CD music. See the consumer web site www.mp3.com. At the time of writing, MP4, even faster to download was being developed.

MUDs Multi-user dungeons, interactive chat-based fantasy world games. Popular in the early days of the internet, they are in now in decline with the advance of games such as Quake and Unreal.

navigate To click on the hyperlinks on a web site in order to move to other web pages or internet sites.

net A slang term for the internet. In the same way, the world wide web is often just called the web.

netiquette Popular term for the unofficial rules and language people follow to keep electronic communication in an acceptably polite form.

Glossary of internet terms ....

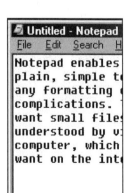

Netmeeting This Microsoft plug in allows a moving video picture to be contained within a web page. It is now integrated into Windows Media Player.

Netscape After Microsoft's Internet Explorer, Netscape is the most popular browser software available for surfing the internet. An excellent product, Netscape has suffered in the wake of Internet Explorer, mainly because of the success of Microsoft in getting the latter pre-loaded on most new PCs. Netscape Communicator comes complete with email, newsgroups, address book and bookmarks, plus a web page composer, and you can adjust its settings in all sorts of useful ways. Netscape was taken over by American Online for $4 billion.

newbie Popular term for a new member of a newsgroup or mailing list.

newsgroup A Usenet discussion group. Each newsgroup is a collection of messages, usually unedited and not checked by anyone ('unmoderated'). Messages can be placed within the newsgroup by anyone including you. It is rather like reading and sending public emails. The ever-growing newsgroups have been around for much longer than the world wide web, and are an endless source of information, gossip, news, entertainment, sex, politics, resources and ideas. The 80,000-plus newsgroups are collectively referred to as Usenet, and millions of people use it every day.

newsreader A type of software that enables you to search, read, post and manage messages in a newsgroup. It will normally be supplied by your internet service provider when you first sign up, or preloaded on your new computer. The best known are Microsoft Outlook, and Netscape Messenger.

news server A remote computer (e.g. your internet service provider) that enables you to access newsgroups. If you cannot get some or any newsgroups from your existing news server, use your favourite search engine to search for 'open news servers' – there are lots of them freely available. When you have found one you like, add it to your news reader by clicking on its name. The first time you do this, it may take 10 to 20 minutes to load the names of all the newsgroups onto your computer, but after that they open up in seconds whenever you want them.

nick Nickname, an alias you can give yourself and use when entering a chat channel, rather than using your real name.

Nominet The official body for registering domain names in the UK (for example web sites whose name ends in .co.uk).

Notepad The most basic type of word processor that comes with a Windows PC. To find it, click Start, Programs, then Accessories. Its more powerful cousin is Wordpad.

online The time you spend linked via a modem to the internet. You can keep your phone bill down by reducing online time. The opposite term is offline.

open source software A type of freely modifiable software, such as Linux. A definition and more information can be found at: http://www.opensource.org

OS The operating system in a computer, for example MS DOS (Microsoft Disk Operating System), or Windows 95/98.

packet The term for any small piece of data sent or received over the internet on your behalf by your internet service provider, and containing your address and the recipient's address. One email message for example may be transmitted as several different packets of information, reassembled at the other end to recreate the message.

parking Placing your web domain into storage until you want to use it at a later date.

password A word or series of letters and numbers that enables a user to access a file, computer or program. A passphrase is a password made by using more than one word.

patch A small piece of software used to patch up a hole or defect ('bug') in a software program.

PC Personal computer, based on IBM technology. It is distinct from the Apple Macintosh which uses a different operating system

PDA Personal Data Assistant – a mobile phone, palm top or any other hand-held processor, typically used to access the internet.

PDF Portable document format, a handy type of file produced using Adobe Acrobat software. It has universal applications for text and graphics.

Pentium The name of a very popular microprocessor chip in personal computers, manufactured by Intel. The first Pentium IIIs were supplied with secret and unique personal identifiers, which ordinary people surfing the net were unwittingly sending out, enabling persons unknown to construct detailed user profiles. After a storm of protest, Pentium changed the technology so that this identifier could be disabled. If you buy or use a Pentium III computer you should be aware of this risk to your privacy when online.

Passwords

ping You can use a ping test to check the connection speed between your computer and another computer.

PGP Pretty Good Privacy. A proprietary method of encoding a message before transmitting it over the internet. With PGP, a message is first compressed then encoded with the help of keys. Just like the valuables in a locked safe, your message is safe unless a person has access to the right keys. Many governments would like complete access to people's private keys. New Labour wanted access to everyone's keys in the UK, but dropped the proposed legislation after widespread protests. Unlike in many countries, there is no general right to privacy in the UK.

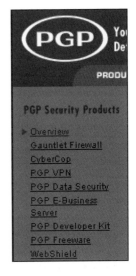

ping You can use a ping test to check the connection speed between your computer and another computer.

plug in A type of (usually free and downloadable) software required to add some form of functionality to web page viewing. A well-known example is Macromedia Shockwave, a plug in which enables you to view animations.

PoP Point of presence. This refers to the dial-up phone numbers available from your ISP. If your ISP does not have a local point of presence (i.e. local access phone number), then don't sign up – your telephone bill will rocket because you will be charged national phone rates. All the major ISPs have local numbers covering the whole of the country.

portal site Portal means gateway. It is a web site designed to be used as a 'home base' from which you can start your web experience each time you go online. Portals often serve as general information points and offer news, weather and other information that you can customise to your own needs. Yahoo! is a good example of a portal (http://www.yahoo.com). A portal site includes the one that loads into your browser each time you connect to the internet. It could for example be the front page of your internet service provider. Or you can set your browser to make it some other front page, for example a search engine such as Yahoo!, or even your own home page if you have one.

post, to The common term used for sending ('posting') messages to a newsgroup. Posting messages is very like sending emails, except of course that they are public and everyone can read them. Also, newsgroup postings are archived, and can be read by anyone in the world years later. Because of this, many people feel more comfortable using an 'alias' (made-up name) when posting messages.

privacy You have practically no personal privacy online. Almost every mouse click and key stroke you make while online may be electronically logged, analysed and possibly archived by internet organisations, government agencies, police or other surveillance services. You are also leaving a permanent trail of data on your computer. But then, if you have nothing to hide you have nothing to fear – or have you? To explore privacy issues worldwide visit the authoritative Electronic Frontier Foundation web site at http://www.eff.org, and for the UK, http://www.netfreedom.org.

program A series of coded instructions designed to automatically control a computer in carrying out a specific task. Programs are written in special languages including Java, JavaScript, VBScript, and ActiveX.

protocol Technical term for the method by which computers communicate. A protocol is something that has been agreed and can be used between systems. For example, for viewing web pages your computer would use hypertext transfer protocol (http). For downloading and uploading files, it would use file transfer protocol (ftp). It's not something to worry too much about in ordinary life.

proxy An intermediate computer or server, used for reasons of security.

Quicktime A popular free software program from Apple Computers. It is designed to play sounds and images including video clips and animations on both Apple Macs and personal computers.

radio button A button that, when clicked, looks like this: ◉

refresh, reload The refresh or reload button on your browser toolbar tells the web page you are looking at to reload.

register You may have to give your name, personal details and financial information to some sites before you can continue to use the pages. Site owners may want to produce a mailing list to offer you products and services. Registration is also used to discourage casual traffic.

registered user Someone who has filled out an online form and then been granted permission to access a restricted area of a web site. Access is usually obtained by logging on, typically by entering a password and user name.

remailer A remailer preserves your privacy by acting as a go-between when you browse or send email messages. An anonymous remailer is simply a computer connected to the internet that can forward an email message to other people after stripping off the header of the messages. Once a message is routed through an anonymous remailer, the recipient of that message, or anyone intercepting it, can no longer identify its origin.

RFC Request for comment. RFCs are the way that the internet developers propose changes and discuss standards and procedures. See http://rs.internic.net.

RSA One of the most popular methods of encryption, and used in Netscape browsers. See http://www.rsa.com.

router A machine that direct internet data (network packets) from one internet location to another.

rules The term for message filters in Outlook Express.

script A script is a set of commands written into the HTML tags of a web page. Script languages such as JavaScript and VBScript work in a similar way to macros in a word processor. Scripts are hidden from view but are executed when you open a page or click a link containing script instructions.

scroll, scroll bar To scroll means to move part of a page or document into view or out of view on the scree. Scrolling is done by using a scroll bar activated by the mouse pointer. Grey scroll bars automatically appear on the right and/or lower edge of the screen if the page contents are too big to fit into view.

search engine A search engine is a web site you can use for finding something on the internet. The technology variously involves the use of 'bots' (search robots), spiders or crawlers. Popular search engines have developed into big web sites and information centres in their own right. There are hundreds of them. Among the best known are AltaVista, Excite, Infoseek, Lycos, Meta-search and Webcrawler. See also **internet directories**.

secure servers The hardware and software provided so that people can use their credit cards and leave other details without the risk of others seeing them online. Your browser will tell you when you are entering a secure site.

secure sockets layer (SSL) A standard piece of technology which ensures secure financial transactions and data flow over the internet.

security certificate Information that is used by the SSL protocol to establish a secure connection. Security certificates contain information about who it belongs to, who it was issued by, some form of unique identification, valid dates, and an encrypted fingerprint that can be used to verify the contents of the certificate.

server Any computer on a network that provides access and serves information to other computers.

shareware Software that you can try before you buy. Usually there is some kind of limitation such as an expiry date. To get the registered version, you must pay for the software, typically $20 to $40. A vast amount of shareware is now available on the internet.

Shockwave A popular piece of software produced by Macromedia, which enables you to view animations and other special effects on web sites. You can download it free and in a few minutes from Macromedia's web site. The effects can be fun, but they slow down the speed at which the pages load into your browser window.

signature file This is a little text file in which you can place your address details, for adding to email and newsgroup messages. Once you have created a signature file, it is appended automatically to your emails. You can of course delete or edit it.

Slashdot One of the leading technology news web sites, found at: http://slash-dot.org

smiley A form of **emoticon**.

snail mail The popular term for the standard postal service involving post-persons, vans, trains, planes, sacks and sorting offices.

sniffer A program on a computer system (usually an ISP's system) designed to collect information. Sniffers are often used by hackers to harvest passwords and user names.

spam The popular term for electronic junk mail – unsolicited and unwelcome email messages sent across the internet. There are various forms of spam-busting software which you can now obtain to filter out unwanted email messages.

SSL Secure socket layer, a key part of internet security technology.

subscribe The term for accessing a newsgroup in order to read and post messages in the newsgroup. There is no charge, and you can subscribe, unsubscribe and resubscribe at will with a click of your mouse. Unless you post a message, no-one in the newsgroup will know that you have subscribed or unsubscribed.

surfing Slang term for browsing the internet, especially following trails of links on pages across the world wide web.

sysop Systems operator, someone rather like a moderator for example of a chat room or bulletin board service.

talkers Servers which give users the opportunity to talk to each other. You connect to them, take a 'nickname' and start chatting. Usually, they offer some other features besides just allowing users to talk to each other, including Bulletin Boards, a 'world' such as a city or building, which you move around in. an opportunity to store some information on yourself, and some games.

TCP/IP Transmission control protocol/internet protocol, the essential technology of the internet. It's not normally something to worry about.

telnet Software that allows you to connect via the internet to a remote computer and work as if you were a terminal linked to that system.

theme A term in web page design. A theme describes the general colours and graphics used within a web site. Many themes are available in the form of readymade templates.

thread An ongoing topic in a Usenet newsgroup or mailing list discussion. The term refers to the original message on a particular topic, and all the replies and other messages which spin off from it. With news reading software, you can easily 'view thread' and thus read the related messages in a convenient batch.

thumbnail A small version of a graphic file which, when clicked, displays a larger size.

top level domain The last code in the domain name, such as .com or .uk

traceroute A program that traces the route from your machine to a remote system. It is useful if you need to discover a person's ISP, for example in the case of a spammer.

traffic The amount of data flowing across the internet, to a particular web site, newsgroup or chat room, or as emails.

trojan horse A program that seems to perform a useful task but is really a malevolent program designed to cause damage to a computer system.

UNIX This is a computer operating system that has been in use for many years, and still is used in many larger systems. Most ISPs use it.

uploading The act of copying files from your PC to a server or other PC on the internet, for example when you are publishing your own web pages. The term is most commonly used to describe the act of copying HTML pages onto the internet via FTP.

URL Uniform resource locator – the address of each internet page. For instance the URL of Internet Handbooks is http://www.internet-handbooks.co.uk

Usenet The collection of over 80,000 active newsgroups that make up a substantial part of the internet.

virtual reality The presentation of a lifelike scenario in electronic form. It can be used for gaming, business or educational purposes.

virtual server A portion of a PC that is used to host your own web domain (if you have one).

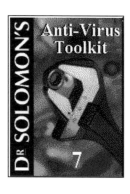

virus A computer program maliciously designed to cause havoc to people's computer files. Viruses can typically be received when downloading program files from the internet, or from copying material from infected disks. Even Word files can now be infected. You can protect yourself from the vast majority of them by installing some inexpensive anti-virus software, such as Norton, McAfee or Dr Solomon.

web authoring Creating HTML pages to upload onto the internet. You will be a web author if you create your own home page for uploading onto the internet.

web Short for the world wide web. See **WWW** below.

WAP Wireless Application Protocol, new technology that enables mobile phones to access the internet.

web-based chat A form of internet chat which is conducted just using web pages, and not requiring special software like IRC and ICQ. For web-based chat, your browser must be Java-enabled. Most modern browsers are Java-enabled by default.

web client Another term for a browser.

Webcrawler A popular internet search engine used to find pages relating to specific keywords entered.

webmaster Any person who manages a web site.

web page Any single page of information you can view on the world wide web. A typical web page includes a unique URL (address), headings, text, images, and hyperlinks (usually in the form of graphic icons, or underlined text). One web page usually contains links to lots of other web pages, either within the same web site or elsewhere on the world wide web.

web ring A network of interlinked web sites that share a common interest.

web site A set of web pages, owned or managed by the same person or organisation, and which are interconnected by hyperlinks.

Whois A network service that allows you to consult a database containing information about someone. A whois query can, for example, help to find the identity of someone who is sending you unwanted email messages.

Windows The ubiquitous operating system for personal computers developed by Bill Gates and the Microsoft Corporation. The Windows 3.1 version was followed by Windows 95, further enhanced by Windows 98. Windows 2000 is the latest.

wizard A feature of many software programs that guides you through its main stages, for example with the use of readymade templates.

WWW The world wide web. Since it began in 1994 this has become the most popular part of the internet. The web is now made up of more than a billion web pages of every imaginable description, typically linking to other pages. Developed by the British computer scientist, Tim Berners-Lee, its growth has been exponential and looks set to continue so.

WYSIWYG 'What you see is what you get.' If you see it on the screen, then it should look just the same when you print it out.

Yahoo! Probably the world's most popular internet directory and search engine, and now valued on Wall Street at billions of dollars: http://www.yahoo.com

zip/unzip Many files that you download from the internet will be in compressed format, especially if they are large files. This is to make them quicker to download. These files are said to be zipped or compressed. Unzipping these compressed files means returning them to their original size ready for use. Zip files have the extension '.zip' and are created (and unzipped) using WinZip or a similar popular software package.

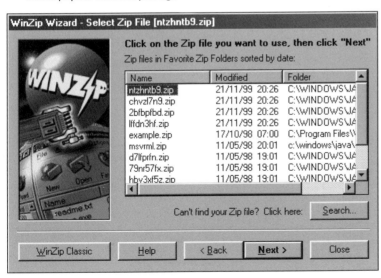

Index

Index. . . . .

1001 Web Sites for Writers
Nick Daws BSc (Hons)

This handy guide offers what all writers on the net really want – a comprehensive list of web sites relevant to their needs and interests. Each chapter contains a short introduction followed by an alphabetically arranged list of web sites relevant to the topic in question. The web sites deal with such topics as grammar, spelling & punctuation, fiction writing, writing for performance, journalism, research, writers' organisations and communities, writing resources and software, the writing life, publishers sites, and sites by and about writers. Each entry summarises what the site offers. The book includes a list of internet access providers, further reading and reference, and an alphabetical index.
1 84025 322 3

Books & Publishing on the Internet
An essential guide for authors, readers, editors, booksellers, librarians & publishing professionals
Roger Ferneyhough MA (Oxon)

Are you an author, bookseller, publisher or editor? Here is a guide to today's whole new world of books and publishing information online. The book reviews web sites of every imaginable kind – of publishers, bookstores, writers' groups, literary agents, book fairs, book distributors, training organisations, prizes, book-related associations, pressure groups, periodicals and many more. Whether you are planning to write, edit, publish or distribute a book, or want to contact a specialist, this is the book for you.
1 84025 332 0

Building a Web Site on the Internet
A practical guide to writing and commissioning web pages
Brendan Murphy BSc (Hons)

The rise in interest in the internet, and especially the word wide web, has been phenomenal. This book meets the urgent need for all business users who need an effective internet presence. Written in plain English, it explains the three main ways of achieving this: create it yourself by writing HTML, create it yourself by using a popular software package, or create it by hiring a web development company. Whether your organisation is large or small, make sure *you* make the right choices for your web site. Brendan Murphy BSc MBA MBSC teaches HNC in Computing, and lectures for the Open University (Course T171, You, Your computer and the Net). He is a Member of the British Computer Society, and Institute of Management Information Systems.
1 84025 314 2

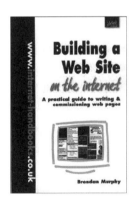

Other Internet Handbooks ....

Careers Guidance on the Internet
An essential guide to careers and vocational guidance resources online
Laurel Alexander MIPD MICG

Are you planning to apply for a new job, or seeking promotion, or looking for new skills? Could you benefit from some vocational guidance, advice or training? Perhaps you are responsible for providing careers guidance to adults or young people? Careers information – like so many other things – is being challenged and revolutionised by the internet. New internet knowledge and skills are urgently needed by every professional working in this vital field. Packed with expert advice, and concise reviews of key web sites, this timely new book will help you take full advantage of some amazing new online resources.
1 84025 351 7

Chat & Chat Rooms on the Internet
A practical guide to exploring the live net chat communities
Mark Ray MSc

Whether you're a recent entrant into the internet world, an experienced web user, or even a dedicated operator of an Internet Relay Chat channel, this book provides an in-depth guide to talkers and IRC. It includes detailed snapshots of real online conversations, information on the major networks, and explains how to download and use the tested client software. Written with the help of some of those who make up these new communities, it also looks at how some have organised themselves into virtual democracies, how they are developing, and discusses where all this fantastic new technology may lead. Use this book, and discover how to start using and enjoying these amazing new possibilities for yourself.
1 84025 347 9

Creating a Home Page on the Internet
An illustrated step-by-step guide for beginners
Richard Cochrane BA(Hons) PhD

Have you just started to use the internet? Or perhaps you are still wondering whether to take the plunge? Either way, you will soon be wondering how you can produce and publish web pages of your own, as millions of other individuals have done all over the world. It's easy! Discover how to design a simple but effective home page; see how to add your own artwork and photographs; learn how to add those magic hypertext links that enable you to click effortlessly from one web page to another. Finally, explore how you can actually publish your own home pages in cyberspace, where potentially anyone in the world can pay you a 'visit' and contact you by email.
1 84025 309 6

Discussion Forums on the Internet
A practical step-by-step guide to newsgroups, mailing lists and bulletin board services
Kye Valongo

With a staggering 80,000 different newsgroups now available, Usenet is one of the most established and popular parts of the internet. A vast number of new messages are posted into newsgroups, mailing lists and bulletin board services every day, and millions of people all over the world love to read them. These forums cover every imaginable subject, from local interest to jobs and travel, education, finance, entertainment, raunchy sex and scandal, culture and politics, computing and more. But how do you access them? Are they censored? How do you read the messages, and post messages yourself? Written in plain English, this guide tells you everything you need to know to explore this lively and ever controversial side of the internet.
1 84025 329 0

Education & Training on the Internet
An essential resource for students, teachers, and education providers
Laurel Alexander MIPD MICG

Can't find the information you want? Confused by search engines? Fed up with floods of irrelevant information? Need to save time and money online? Then here is a truly amazing resource, a guide to today's exploding new world of education and training online. Here are web sites of every imaginable kind – for education and training providers, schools, colleges, universities, training centres, professional organisations, resource suppliers, individuals, business organisations and academic institutions. Whether you are planning to study online, or are planning the delivery of online education and training, you will find this a key resource.
1 84025 346 0

Exploring Yahoo! on the Internet
A practical guide for internet users everywhere
David Holland ACIB

Yahoo! is one of the two or three most popular web sites on the internet. This practical guide shows you how to get the most out of Yahoo! as an information resource, how to track down over a billion web pages and a vast range of other internet services, using its highly developed local and international search features. But today Yahoo! is much more than just a vast internet directory and search engine. You can use it as a communications tool complete with address book, messaging, email, chat, and greetings services, which you can personalise with your own bookmarks, investment, news and weather updates. You can even get Yahoo! on your mobile phone. The book also explores shopping with Yahoo! including auctions, a business finder, property, classifieds, and communities such as Clubs and Geocities.
1 84025 323 1

Other Internet Handbooks...

Finding a Job on the Internet
Amazing new possibilities for jobseekers everywhere
Brendan Murphy BSc (Hons)

Thinking of looking for a new job, or even a change of career? The internet is a really great place to start your job search. In easy steps and plain English, this new Internet handbook explains how to find and use internet web sites and newsgroups to give you what you need. School, college and university leavers will find it a valuable resource for identifying suitable employers and getting expert help with CVs and job applications. The book will also be useful for employers thinking of using the internet for recruitment purposes, and for career and training advisers everywhere.
1 84025 365 7 (second edition)

Gardens & Gardening on the Internet
A practical handbook and reference guide to horticulture online
Judith & Graham Lawlor MA

Gardeners are often in need of specific information to help them in their projects, and the internet is proving an amazingly valuable new aid to modern gardening. This new book leads you quickly and painlessly to some amazing new gardening help lines, retail and wholesale suppliers, online clubs and societies, and web sites devoted to such topics as rare plants, water gardens, celebrity gardening, gardening holidays, and horticultural science. The book will be absolutely indispensable for all gardeners with access to the internet.
1 84025 313 4.

Getting Started on the Internet
A practical step-by-step guide for beginners
Kye Valongo

Confused by search engines, worried about email, baffled by browsers? In plain English, this beginner's guide takes you gently step-by-step through all the basics of the internet. It shows you how to obtain free access to the internet, how to set up your computer, how to look for information, and how to send and receive emails. It explains how to explore newsgroups and internet chat, how to protect your privacy online, and even how to create your own home page. Whether you want the internet for use at home, in education or in the workplace, this is the book for you, specially designed to get you up and running with the minimum fuss and bother.
1 84025 321 5

Graduate Job Hunting on the Internet
A practical illustrated guide for all university and college leavers
Laurel Alexander MIPD MICG

Are you a graduate looking for work? The internet is now by far the easiest way to search for the type of job you want. In a quick and easy format, this book will provide you with everything you need to find the right job in the UK or abroad. Discover how you can keep ahead of the competition by gaining employability skills, where the growth areas of industry and commerce are and how you can always have an income. More than 300 essential sites are reviewed, covering areas such as graduate recruitment agencies, graduate employers and overseas graduate placements. Additional sections provide resources for careers advice, company research, vocational training and job search. Use this book and make sure you are up to speed!
1 84025 361 4

Homes & Property on the Internet
A guide to 1000s of top web sites for buyers, sellers, owners, tenants, sharers, holiday makers & property professionals
Philip Harrison

Here is a guide to today's whole new world of homes and property services online. Here are web sites of every imaginable kind for estate agents, house builders, removal firms, decorators, town planners, architects and surveyors, banks and building societies, home shares, villa owners and renters, and property-related associations, pressure groups, newspapers and magazines. Whether you are planning to move house, or rent a holiday home, or locate property services in the UK or wider afield, this is the book for you – comprehensive and well-indexed to help you find what you want.
1 84025 335 5

Law & Lawyers on the Internet
An essential guide and resource for legal practitioners
Stephen Hardy JP LLB PhD

Legal practitioners, law firms, judges, the courts and litigants are now recognising the value of technology in legal research, administration and practice. Following the Woolf Reforms, efficient research and communication will be the key to future legal life. This handbook will meet the needs of solicitors, barristers, law students, public officials, community groups and consumers alike who are seeking guidance on how to access and use the major legal web sites and information systems available to them on the internet. It includes expert site reviews on law associations, law firms, case law and court reporting, European legal institutions, government, legal education and training, publishers, the courts and branches of the law. Don't leave for court without it!
1 84025 345 2

Marketing Your Business on the Internet (2nd edition)
A practical step-by-step guide for all business owners and managers
Sara Edlington

Is your business online? Or perhaps you are still debating whether to take the plunge? For many businesses, the internet will become an essential tool over the next few years, for reaching the vast new online markets for all kinds of goods and services. Written by someone experienced in marketing on the internet from its earliest days, this practical book will show you step-by-step how to make a success of marketing your organisation on the internet. Discover how to find a profitable on-line niche, know which ten essential items to have on your web site, how to keep visitors returning again and again, how to secure valuable on- and off-line publicity for your organisation, and how to build your brand online. The internet is set to create phenomenal new marketing opportunities – make sure you are ready to win your share.
1 84025 364 9 (2nd edition)

Medicine & Health on the Internet
A practical guide to online advice, treatments, doctors and support groups
Sarah Wilkinson

In the last couple of years, thousands of new health and medical web sites have been launched on the internet. Do you want to find out about a specialist treatment or therapy? Do you want to contact a support group or clinician online, or perhaps just get the answer to a simple question? Don't get lost using search engines. Whether you are a patient, relative, carer, doctor, health administrator, medical student or nurse, this book will lead you quickly to all the medical and health resources you need – help lines, support groups, hospitals, clinics and hospices, health insurance and pharmaceutical companies, treatments, suppliers, professional bodies, journals, and more.
1 84025 340 1

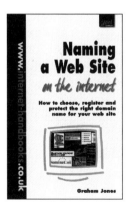

Naming a Web Site on the Internet
How to choose, register and protect the right domain name for your web site
Graham Jones BSc (Hons)

Would you like to obtain a proper domain name for your own web site, for example 'dot.com' or 'dot.co.uk'? Perhaps you have a name in mind, but are not sure how to register it. Do you know the rules which govern the naming of web sites? This valuable handbook explains just how to choose and register your own 'domain name' on the world wide web. The official rules are clearly explained, with lots of practical examples to help you. There are many places you can apply for a domain name and a bewildering array of prices and conditions. This book provides a clear step-by-step guide through the maze. It also explains how to protect your domain names, where to 'host' them, and how to move them from one machine to another. The rush is on – act now to register and protect the names you want.
1 84025 359 2

News & Magazines on the Internet
A practical guide to newspapers, magazines, radio, and other online news and information services
Michael Newman

Here is a truly amazing resource – a handy guide to today's new world of internet newspapers, e-zines, press agencies, newsfeeds, radio and TV broadcasters, and a huge array of other news services online. Discover how to access newspapers and magazines in almost any country. Browse through the *New York Times* or *Wall Street Journal*. Get the latest news and background about politics, sport, finance and entertainment, anywhere from Paris and Berlin to Sydney or Bangkok. Arrange for customised news to be downloaded to your desktop or laptop. Find out what's happening just about anywhere on the planet. Whether you are a media student, teacher, sports fan, pundit, politician or journalist, this book will speed you to all the news and updates you need.
1 84025 342 8

Overseas Job Hunting on the Internet
A practical illustrated guide for everyone seeking employment overseas
Laurel Alexander MIPD MICG

The internet gives you global opportunities for employment and this book will tell you all you need to know to find a great job anywhere in the world. Discover how you can apply for permanent, temporary and contract work. You will find more than 300 top web sites in this book, detailing UK recruitment agencies for overseas work, international recruitment agencies, professional organisations that recruit overseas and companies that recruit overseas. There are also sections on voluntary work overseas, relocation services, embassies and government bodies plus international legislation.
1 84025 366 5

Personal Finance on the Internet
Your complete online guide to savings, investment, loans, mortgages, pensions, insurance and all aspects of personal finance
Graham Jones BSc (Hons)

For many people the internet is now the preferred means of managing their personal finances. But how do you do it? Where can you check out financial products and services on the internet? How secure is it, and what are the risks? Step-by-step this book describes the emerging world of online personal finance. It explains what you need to run your finances on the internet, where to find financial information, managing your bank account online, getting credit via the internet, checking out mortgages online, saving your money online, buying and selling stocks and shares online, arranging your pensions and insurance online, paying taxes, and much more.
1 84025 320 7

Other Internet Handbooks ....

Promoting a Web Site on the Internet

A practical guide to attracting visitors using traditional and online techniques
Graham Jones BSc (Hons)

Do you know how to get your web site listed by the main search engines? Should you pay people to promote your web site? What are banner ads and web rings? This book shows you step-by-step how to plan and carry out the promotion of a new web site. It explains how to use the main search engines and internet indexes, how to use commercial services to get your web site noticed, and how to track down and use various new kinds of cooperative online help. Why not use traditional promotion methods, too? Surprisingly few internet operators use media such as print, mail or radio to promote their web sites. Yet traditional methods reach a wider public and can bring your site to the attention of a huge audience. This book shows you how to maximise both new and traditional promotional techniques, to give your new site the best chance of success.
1 84025 354 1

Protecting Children on the Internet

An effective approach for parents and teachers
Graham Jones BSc (Hons)

Are you concerned that children in your care might view unsuitable material on the internet? Without the right protection, children can easily stumble across pornography, violence, sexism, racism, and other damaging material. This book tells you step-by-step how to make sure that your youngsters are free to get the best from the internet, whilst shielding them from the worst. Using practical examples, it explains how to set up your web browser to protect them, how to use parental controls and filtering software to exclude unwelcome content from your child's screen, and so ensure a positive experience of this powerful new medium.
1 84025 344 4

Shops & Shopping on the Internet

A practical guide to online stores, catalogues, retailers and shopping malls
Kathy Lambert

In the last couple of years, thousands of shops and stores have been launched on the internet. But what are they like? Where can you find your favourite brands and stores? What about deliveries from suppliers in the UK or overseas? Can you safely pay by credit card? Don't get stuck in the internet traffic! This carefully structured book will take you quickly to all the specialist stores, virtual shopping malls, and online catalogues of your choice. You will be able to compare prices, and shop till you drop for books, magazines, music, videos, clothes, holidays, electrical goods, games and toys, wines, and a vast array of other goods and services.
1 84025 327 4

Studying English on the Internet
An A to Z guide to useful electronic resources freely available on the internet
Wendy Shaw

Written by a university researcher, this new guide has been specially collated for the internet user of all levels in the discipline of English. Whether you are a student, teacher, tutor or lecturer, this is the guide for you. It offers a clear and graphical presentation of web sites and electronic resources on the internet for both teaching and research purposes. The A-Z format makes it easy to pick out an author or electronic text centre from the bulleted list. Hundreds of key gateway web sites for English Studies are reviewed in this valuable course companion.
1 84025 317 7

Studying Law on the Interent
How to use the internet for learning and study, exams and career development
Stephen Hardy JP LLB PhD

Are you studying law at college or university, or as a distance learner? Do you have internet access? Computers and the internet are becoming ever more important in both legal learning and practice today. The internet in particular is a place of rich legal resource, for barristers, solicitors, legal executives and officials alike. This handbook meets the needs of law students wanting quick access to the major relevant legal web sites and legal information systems available over the internet. Use this book to expand your knowledge, develop your skills, and greatly improve your career prospects.
1 84025 370 3

The Internet for Schools
A practical step-by-step guide for teachers, student teachers, parents and governors
Barry Thomas & Richard Williams

This title is aimed at teachers, student teachers, parents and school governors – in fact anyone interested in using the internet in primary and secondary education. The format is entertaining with key points highlighted. Each chapter is free-standing and should take no more than fifteen minutes to read. A major aim is to explain things in clear, non-technical and non-threatening language. There are detailed reviews of many key educational internet sites. The book is UK focused, and contains typical examples and practical tasks that could be undertaken with students.
1 84025 302 9

Other Internet Handbooks ....

The Internet for Students
Making the most of the new medium for study and fun
David Holland ACIB

Are you a student needing help with the internet to pursue your studies? Not sure where to start? – then this Internet Handbook is the one for you. It's up to date, full of useful ideas of places to visit on the internet, written in a clear and readable style, with plenty of illustrations and the minimum of jargon. It is the ideal introduction for all students who want to add interest to their studies, and make their finished work stand out, impressing lecturers and future employers alike. The internet is going to bring about enormous changes in modern life. As a student, make sure you are up to speed.
1 84025 306 1 – Reprinted

The Internet for Writers
Using the new medium to research, promote and publish your work
Nick Daws BSc (Hons)

This guide offers all writers with a complete introduction to the internet – how to master the basic skills, and how to use this amazing new medium to create, publish and promote your creative work. Would you like to broaden and speed up your research? Meet fellow writers, editors and publishers through web sites, newsgroups, or chat? Even publish your work on the internet for a potentially enormous new audience? Then this is the book you need, with all the practical starting points to get you going, step by step. The book is a selection of *The UK Good Book Guide*.
1 84025 308 8

Travel & Holidays on the Internet
The amazing new world of online travel services, information, prices, reservations, timetables, bookings and more
Graham Jones BSc (Hons)

Thinking of checking out flights to Europe or America, or booking a package holiday? The internet is the best place to start. In easy steps and plain English, this book explains how to find and use the web to locate the travel and holiday information you need. You can view the insides of hotels, villas and even aeroplanes, quickly compare costs and services, and make your reservations and bookings securely online. All the big holiday and travel companies are now online – from airlines to the major tour operators but you'll be amazed at how much more you'll find with the help of this remarkable book.
1 84025 325 8

Using Credit Cards on the Internet
A practical step-by-step guide for all cardholders and retailers
Graham Jones BSc (Hons)

Are you worried about using credit cards on the internet? Do you know the truth about 'secure transactions'? Would you like to know how to get a special online credit card? This valuable new book shows you how to avoid trouble and use your 'virtual plastic' in complete safety over the internet. It contains all the low-down on security, practical tips to make sure that all your credit card dealings are secure, and advice on where to find credit cards with extra 'web protection'. It also show how to apply online for a new credit card, and how to use certain other forms of payments now widely accepted over the internet. If you are running a business on the internet, it also explains how to set up a 'merchant account' so that customers can safely pay you using their credit cards. The book is complete with a guide to the best sites on credit card usage.
1 84025 349 5

Using Email on the Internet
A step-by-step guide to sending and receiving messages and files
Kye Valongo

Email is one of the oldest parts of the internet. Most newcomers approach it with a bit of trepidation. But don't worry – it is quite straightforward and easy. By the time you have finished reading this book you will be happily sending emails across the world and not even flinching. Emailing is fast, cheap and convenient, and you'll soon wonder how you ever managed without it. Use this book to find out how to get started, how to successfully send and receive your first messages, how to send and receive attached files, how to manage your email folders, address book, user profiles, personal privacy, and lots more valuable skills.
1 84025 300 2

Using Netscape on the Internet
A step-by-step guide to using your browser
Kye Valongo

Are you using Netscape Navigator on your computer to browse the internet? This book tells you all about this popular and powerful browser, used by millions of people every day. It shows how to use the built-in email facility, and create several different User Profiles. Learn how to store and organise your favourite web pages as Bookmarks. Discover how to access thousands of controversial newsgroups using Netscape Messenger. Explore the User Preferences, where you can control the cookies and other information about your internet activity stored on your computer. You can even create and publish your own web pages using Netscape Composer. If you use Netscape, you definitely need this book.
1 84025 339 8

Other Internet Handbooks..

Where to Find It on the Internet (2nd edition)
Your complete guide to search engines, portals, databases, yellow pages & other internet reference tools
Kye Valongo

Here is a valuable basic reference guide to hundreds of carefully selected web sites for everyone wanting to track down information on the internet. Don't waste time with fruitless searches – get to the sites you want, fast. This book provides a complete selection of the best search engines, online databases, directories, libraries, people finders, yellow pages, portals, and other powerful research tools. A recent selection of 'The Good Book Guide', and now in a new edition, this book will be an essential companion for all internet users, whether at home, in education, or in the workplace.
1 84025 369 X – 2nd edition

Wildlife & Conservation on the Internet
An essential guide to environmental resources online
Kate Grey BSc(Hons)

Are you interested in the future of our natural heritage? Perhaps you are a student or teacher of environmental studies, or with a job in this responsible area? Here is a unique guide to wildlife trusts, official and public organisations, coastal and marine web sites, nature reserves, zoos, national parks, and thousands more online resources. With its expert reviews, this timely book is essential reference for town and country dwellers, officials and planners, conservationists, and everyone interested in environmental issues. It is also a valuable resource for primary and secondary schools and teachers, and college lecturers, using the internet for educational purposes.
1 84025 318 5

Working from Home on the Internet
A practical illustrated guide for everyone
Laurel Alexander MIPD MICG

Would you like to work from home and earn good money using communications technology and the internet? There is a huge increase in people working from home, either self-employed or as an employee for a company. More than 250 top sites are reviewed in this book which detail business opportunities on the internet, employers who use home workers (including teleworkers) as well as recruitment agencies for IT and internet work. There are also sections on finding capital, legislation for the self employed, support for home workers (including disabled workers), business services and suppliers on the internet (including internet services, business advice and office supplies) and internet-based learning. Get this ground-breaking book – and make sure you are up to speed!
1 84025 371 1

Your Privacy on the Internet
Everything you need to know about protecting your privacy and security on-line
Kye Valongo

Is Big Brother watching you? Many people will be shocked to hear that eavesdropping on private electronic communication is relatively easy and commonplace. This book explores the various ways that governments, companies and hackers are all using the internet to invade your privacy. It then explains the various types of freely available privacy technology you can use to prevent snooping and protect your privacy, whether you are browsing web pages, sending or receiving emails, accessing newsgroups, using search engines, or transmitting or receiving any kind of data online. The new borderless world is fundamentally changing the way we live. Stay alert, and keep ahead.
1 84025 355 X